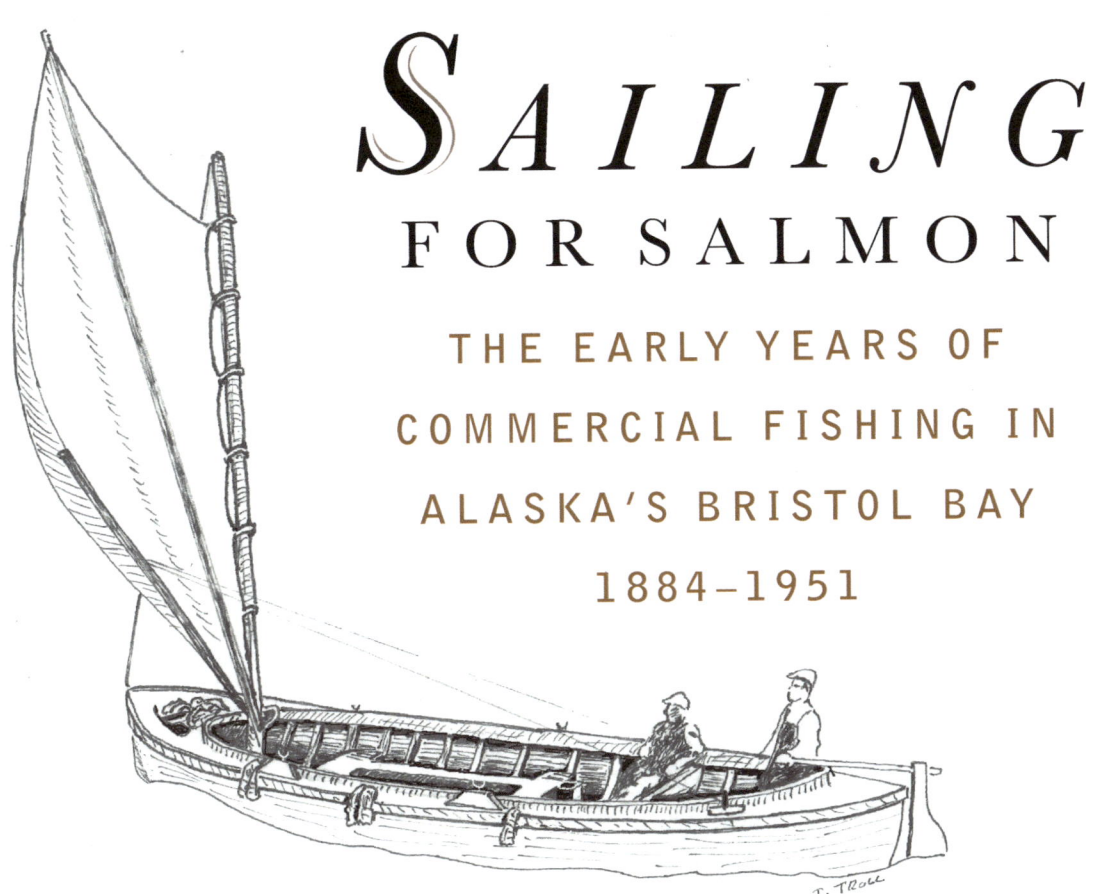

Sailing
For Salmon

THE EARLY YEARS OF
COMMERCIAL FISHING IN
ALASKA'S BRISTOL BAY
1884–1951

Dedication: *To the fishermen and cannery workers from Bristol Bay and around the world who pioneered the greatest salmon fishery on earth.*

Edited and Illustrated by Tim Troll

Design by David Freeman

ACKNOWLEDGEMENTS

The author wishes to express gratitude to John Branson, Historian for the Lake Clark National Park and Preserve and co-curator with the author of the museum exhibit of the same name. Neither this book nor the exhibit could have come into being without his assistance and deep knowledge of the history of Bristol Bay.

Others whose advice, help and inspiration were particularly valuable include Hjalmar Olsen, Melvin Monsen Sr., Robin Samuelsen, Helena Andree, Molly Chythlook, Gusty Bartman, Lyle Smith, Jerry Liboff, Mike Davis, Bob King, Clark James Mishler and Janet Klein.

Funding for *Sailing for Salmon* was provided by the National Park Service, Lake Clark National Park and Preserve, the Alaska Humanities Forum and the National Endowment for the Humanities, a federal agency. Additional support was provided by The Nature Conservancy, the Bristol Bay Heritage Land Trust and the U.S. Fish & Wildlife Service Coastal Program. Any views, findings, conclusions or recommendations expressed in this publication do not represent those of any of these organizations.

© Copyright 2011
Bristol Bay Heritage Land Trust
P.O. Box 1388, Dillingham, AK 99576
(907) 842-2832   Email - bbheritagelt@nushtel.com   Website - www.bristolbaylandtrust.org

ISBN: 978-0-615-47050-4

God, how I wish I could live those days over.

AXEL WIDERSTROM, 1976

Bristol Bay in Southwest Alaska is one of the great commercial fisheries of the world. More than half of the earth's sockeye salmon return to "the Bay" every year. *Sailing for Salmon* is a nostalgic look back, through photographs and recollections, on the sailboat days, a time when these salmon were harvested from sailboats – a time still within living memory. These sailboats, called Bristol Bay double-enders, were well-crafted and beautiful, but obsolete for most of their history. The use of motorized fishing vessels was finally allowed in 1951. The Bristol Bay commercial fishery has changed much since then, but the sailboat remains the iconic image of a fishery born on the wind.

I may be old fashioned, but still believe that it's only those guys who know how to harness the wind who really know how to fish.

JOHN NICHOLSON

FORWARD

Robin H. Samuelsen
Bristol Bay Commercial Fisherman
Chairman of the Board, Bristol Bay Economic Development Corporation

Bristol Bay: The Salmon Capital of the World

In the late 1800's, my great grandfather was a resident at Nushagak, a small village in Bristol Bay. His name was John W. Clark and he had a trading post. He was the one person you went to if you needed to get things done in Bristol Bay before the turn of the last century. John W. was one of the people responsible for starting the commercial fishing industry here in Bristol Bay. He helped build the first cannery at Kanulik in 1883. John W. then went down river and started a cannery at Clarks Point, a village named in his honor. The oldest cannery standing in Bristol Bay today is the Clarks Point cannery. It does not process fish anymore but it is an experience when you walk around it. One can just visualize it operating and processing those salmon, with all those workers. John W. was always helping people.

Robin H. Samuelsen and his grandaughter Peyton

In 1891 he guided some newspapermen to an unknown lake in the Kvichak River drainage, a lake now called Lake Clark. Grandpa Clark was so close to the salmon industry at age 50 he contracted fish poisoning and died. He is buried at Nushagak village.

John W. Clark

"Sailing for Salmon" is what the Bristol Bay salmon fishery is all about. Wooden sailboats were used with a total cost for each boat around $200 These boats were crewed by two people who fished from Monday to Saturday. These men were made of iron. They slept under a canvas tent, cooked all their meals on small coal or gas stoves. Getting and staying wet from the seas was as common as seeing a seagull flying overhead. They pulled their nets in by hand, no hydraulics. My grandpa John W. Nicholson put fifty years in fishing a sailboat in Bristol Bay. He told me time and time again that we should have stayed with the sailboats.

I especially want to thank my father Harvey Samuelsen, who taught me how to fish and how important these salmon are to us in Bristol Bay and the nation. Harvey fished Bristol Bay for fifty years, starting in sailboats, and was a leader for local fishermen up until his death in 2004.

Our salmon enjoy the pure clean waters in our lakes and streams. They return every year in the millions and our fishermen and subsistence users look forward to the spring of each year, setting nets and processing those salmon. The salmon stocks of Bristol Bay provide thousands of jobs for the men and women of Bristol Bay, not to mention folks from the lower 48 and around the world. We must make sure that nothing ever disrupts or pollutes the lakes, rivers and streams that these salmon need to survive on.

The Lord has blessed the land and waters of Bristol Bay, providing us with this sustainable resource second to none—salmon. Hopefully, five hundred years from now we will still be "Sailing for Salmon" here in Bristol Bay with the pride that past and present folks have, providing a healthy source of protein to the people of the world.

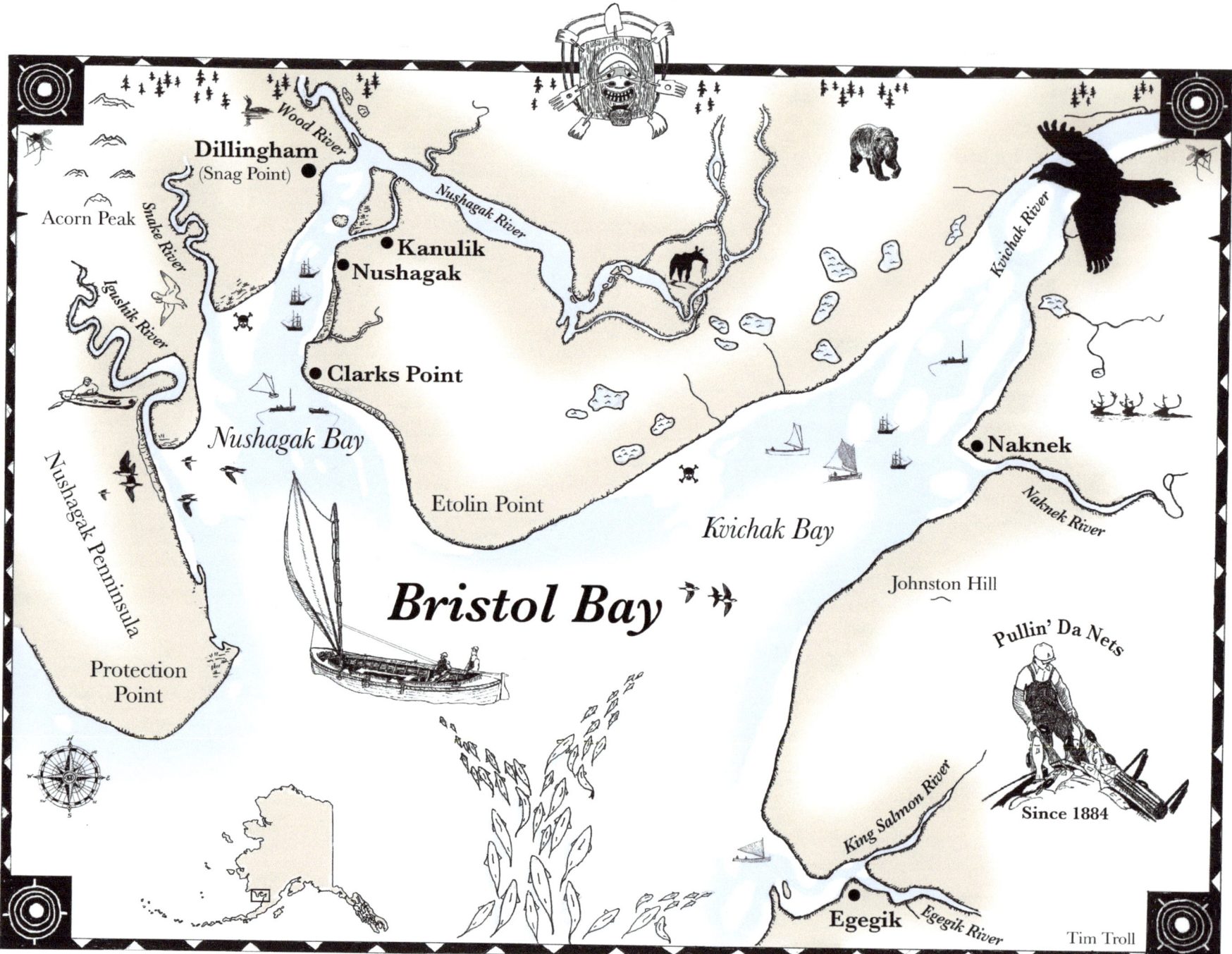

The first cannery in Bristol Bay was built in 1883 at the Yup'ik village of Kanulik on the Nushagak River. The cannery was built by San Francisco businessmen Carl Rohlffs and Henry Fortmann. It began operation in 1884 as the Arctic Packing Company.

This photo, passed down through the family of John W. Clark, shows the cannery not long after it was built. It is provided courtesy of his granddaughter Elizabeth Nicholson Butkovich.

The oldest surviving cannery in Bristol Bay is located at Clarks Point, founded by John W. Clark. Built by San Francisco businessman Louis Sloss in 1888, the Nushagak Canning Company was the fourth cannery built in Bristol Bay. This photo panoramic was taken in 1917 by John Cobb from the cannery water tower looking north toward Nushagak Point. Cobb worked for the Alaska Packers Association and founded the fisheries program at the University of Washington.

"Star of Alaska" sailing for Bristol Bay ca 1910 with cannery workers and fishermen aboard. The 301-foot, square-rigged sailing ship is preserved at the San Francisco Maritime National Historical Park under its original name "Balclutha."

The "Star of India" at anchor off Dillingham (Snag Point) ca 1906. The 278-foot iron hulled "Star of India" is preserved at the Maritime Museum of San Diego and is the oldest ship in the world that still sails regularly. She made 22 voyages to Alaska.

Fishing. It's what's done in Bristol Bay. Some seasons are a bust. In others, the nets are smokin'. Reds everywhere. Canneries plugged. Boats on limit. Biologists scratching their heads. It's been life in "the Bay" for more than one hundred thirty years.

The fishery began in 1884 when San Francisco businessman Carl Rohlffs organized the Arctic Packing Company and built the first cannery on the Bay at the Native village of Kanulik across the Nushagak River from present day Dillingham. The first commercial pack of canned salmon was only about 400 cases or 6000 fish. A meager beginning for what would eventually become the most productive wild salmon fishery in the world.

By 1900 numerous other canneries appeared bringing profound change to this region. In a short time The Bay became an international melting pot as the fishery attracted Scandinavian, Chinese, Japanese, Filipino, Mexican, Italian, English, Irish, and even Inupiat people from Northern Alaska, all of whom mixed with the local Yup'ik, Aleutiq and Athabascan populations to produce one of the most heterogeneous populations in Alaska.

One curious feature that became the iconic image of the Bristol Bay fishery was a federal government mandate that salmon could only be harvested from sailboats. The federal government managed Alaska's fisheries until statehood in 1959.

The 1880's to the early 1950's are known as "the sailboat days" when the wild salmon of Bristol Bay were harvested primarily by the Columbia River type double-ended sailing gillnetter. The boat is commonly known as the "double-ender" because the shape of its bow and stern were similar. The double-ender was a craft of beauty, about 29 feet long, and constructed of rot resistant Port Orford yellow cedar planking shaped by ribs of white oak and an iron bark keel. The beamy but sensual lines of the boat were complemented by the winged shape of its sprit-rigged sail. They were seaworthy boats that could pack a load of fish, frequently 1,500 to 2,000 five to seven pound sockeye salmon. The charm of the double-ender sharply contrasts the iron clad, big power, gadget and gizmo driven gillnetter that dominates commercial fishing in the Bay today.

Charming, however, is not generally the first word that comes to mind when many of the old fishermen described fishing in them. They were work boats and in those days fishing was extremely hard, miserable work. The double-enders were open and exposed to the often cold and wet weather of the Bay. Catching fish in them was arduous. Nets were set and pulled by hand; and the nets, made of water absorbent linen and wax coated wooden floats, were heavy even without fish in them. All of this seems more incredible when you consider that during most of the sailboat days fishing was generally a twenty-four hour a day - six day affair every week. Six days in the rain and the wind. Six days rolling on the waves. Six days sleeping among the scales and fish slime. Six days with only an unshaven, unbathed partner for company. Fishermen got a break on Sunday, but it was back out on Monday for another six days.

Providence made Bristol Bay the motherlode of the world's salmon fisheries, but it did so with a fiendish touch. In addition to being hard work, fishing is also dangerous work and the Bay is one of the most dangerous fishing grounds in the world. To catch fish a Bristol Bay fishermen must negotiate a maze of shallow waters, giant tides, shifting sand bars and wind swept waves. Many fishermen have failed, a good number giving their lives in the effort. The task was especially difficult in a double-ender. Without power or a radio to call for help, a fisherman had to rely on his skill at the sail and tiller or on a strong back at the oars to avert tragedy. Death was always present; the invisible third crewman. No wonder, in the lore of fishing in Bristol Bay the sailing days represent a fabled era - the time of "iron men in wooden boats," in contrast to the post-sailing period of "wooden men in iron boats."

As romantic as the double-ender may have been, it was a craft of servitude. Each cannery owned a fleet of double-enders, decided who would get to fish in them, and towed the boats they owned with the fishermen they chose to the fishing grounds. The politically powerful canneries preserved the double-ender long beyond its obsolescence by securing a Federal law that prohibited the use of motorized fishing craft in Bristol Bay. The law was sugarcoated as a conservation measure, but in fact it was an industry protection measure. Power was finally legalized in 1951. Power bestowed independence on the Fisherman - the ability to move quickly around the fishing grounds and sell to the cannery offering the best price. Motorized power reduced the leverage of the canneries over the fisherman, albeit perhaps only from a stranglehold to a wrist-lock.

Independence from the canneries, however, did not come without a price. Motorized power also made the Bay accessible to a lot more fishermen; and they came. Twenty years after the legalization of power Alaska enacted a limited entry law to fix the number of fishermen allowed to catch fish in order to protect the Bay from overfishing. Nearly fifty years after limited entry was imposed, the Bay is still crowded. For these reasons some old fishermen lament the loss of the double-ender. John Nicholson of Dillingham was one of them. He fished for more than a half century in the Bay. He published a book called "No Half Truths" and in it he was not shy about his opinion. He wrote:

> *The reason I was against power boats was because every Tom, Dick and Harry might fish. After legalization of power and the establishment of Limited Entry it seems there are now twice as many fishermen. These include doctors, lawyers and other professionals; it seemed all the pencil pushers started fishing. During sailboat days, they wouldn't have been able to fish, because they might have been afraid to sail. The rigors of sailing and living in an open boat would have been overwhelming. I may be old fashioned, but I still feel that it's only those guys who know how to harness the wind really know how to fish.*

In the sailing days everybody fished the same gear. The bounty of the fishery went to those with skill, courage and knowledge. Today better gear can make up for a lack of these attributes.

Going back to sailboats may be the answer to the woes of overcrowding in Bristol Bay, but it is not one of the choices available. Perhaps in time market forces or the tenacity of the salmon to defy all predictions will weed out some of the Toms, Dicks and Harrys. Certainly a balance is needed. In the meantime I can't help but wonder what it was like to fish in one of those double-enders. I imagine the sounds that have become extinct - the ripple and then the snap of the sail as the wind brings it taught, the clack of wooden corks spilling over the gunwale, the slap of waves against the cedar hull, or the creak of a bent mast sailing before a brisk wind. Or imagine the sounds that weren't heard - the chug of a diesel engine, the clatter and chat of the VHF radio, and the echo of waves rapping an aluminum hull. Fishing in a sailboat must have been a quiet undertaking. And what about smells like damp wood and wet canvass, or even the smell of sea itself. All gone, replaced by the odor of diesel and gasoline.

And finally there is the vision of sails on the water, dozens of sails, if not hundreds of sails. A sight never to be seen again.

Tim Troll

All gillnet fishermen in Bering Sea to receive fifty dollars ($50.00) as run money. In addition to this each gillnet fisherman shall receive five cents (.05) for each King Salmon weighing over 15 pounds; one and one-half cents (.015) for each Red or Coho Salmon; one-half cent (.005) for each Chum or Dog Salmon; one-half cent (.005) for each Pink Salmon caught and delivered to the company. The Company is not compelled to take any Dog or Pink Salmon, but if received they are to be paid for at the above rates.

Articles of Agreement and Wage Scale for the Season of 1907 between
the various Alaska Salmon Packers and the Alaska Fishermen's Union

The gill net boats used on the Nushagak and the Ugashik are regular Columbia River boats, built in San Francisco at an average price, complete, of $200. The usual dimensions are: Length, 25 feet 1 inch; Beam, 7 feet 8 inches; Depth, 2 feet 6 inches; Capacity, 300 cubic feet. They have a centerboard and spritsail, and will carry, as an extreme, 1,400 redfish. The boats used on the Kvichak, and Naknek, and Egegik are flat-bottom double-enders, about one foot longer than the Columbia River boats, but have the same rig and capacity, and on the water resemble them very closely. Their value is about $100, complete.

JEFFERSON S. MOSER, 1900

When we started building gillnet boats, we got beautiful Port Orford cedar from down the coast and I remember we paid $195 for a thousand board feet, but the last time we tried to buy it was more than $3000 a thousand board feet . . . the Japanese started buying it which made the price go way up. . . We finally switched to Alaska yellow cedar . . . The best of the boat lumber which included mahogany, oak, fir and iron bark as well as the cedar was stored in a dry lumbar shed located at the north end of the shipyard and above this shed was a mold loft which had a large white floor for laying out the full size boat plans.

MEL HJORTEN,
Columbia River Packers Association Astoria, Oregon

Salmon Fishing Boats. Clarks Point. Bristol Bay, Alaska. Thwaites.

They were great sea boats – centerboarders. If it blew too hard they would dispense with the sprit that peaks up the sail. If it was still blowing too hard, they would reef the sail by lashing several of the mast hoops together. Also, there were holes in the sail above the boom that a reefing line could be rove through.

AXEL WIDERSTROM

As the season commenced the boats and nets were readied, fishermen tried to find the lightest weight masts, booms, sprits and oars. Sometimes we shaved our mast down to make it even lighter. Then we'd oil it by rubbing it with a beef knuckle, which would make the sail rings slide easily and drop promptly when released.

AL ANDREE

When we stepped the mast on an older boat early in the season, we always found four or five good luck pennies in the mast step. We always threw in another.

AL ANDREE

"Yarrayulli," Scandanavian fisherman ca 1917. Yup'ik name for Scandinavians - "the ones who always say Yaa."

Fishermen were mostly Italians, Scandinavians and Finns hired at Seattle and San Francisco. The canneries liked Scandinavians from the Lofoten Islands off the coast of Norway, where sailing boats similar to those in Bristol Bay were used, or Italians from Sardinia or the Messina Straits for the same reason.

A cannery superintendent preferred to have a mixture of nationalities for fishermen, and he would deliberately hire Finns, Italians or Scandinavians, telling them, "I know you Finns (or Italians, or Scandinavians) are the best fishermen. I expect you to show those Italians and Scandinavians (or Finns) how to catch salmon."

During the season everyone kept track of which nationality made the best catches. Insults sometimes almost got serious. National pride was an incentive to fish hard.

AL ANDREE

"Yugngalnuq," Yup'ik name for Italians - "the ones who who are darker like us."
Ralph Angilesco, Italian fisherman from San Francisco, 1940.

The Iron Men of Bristol Bay
By Bob King

Sailboat fishermen are often described as the "Iron Men in Wooden Boats." The name honors their hard work in those open boats that lacked the conveniences of motors, hydraulics and cabins.

The Alaska Packers Association (APA) was the largest of Bristol Bay's historic salmon canners and archives at the Center for Pacific Northwest Studies in Bellingham hold several boxes of 4 by 6-inch cards: the company's records of their Bristol Bay fishermen from 1908 to 1941. They paint a vivid picture of the fishermen who caught sockeye during the Bay's sailboat era.

Most of these fishermen were immigrants: Europeans from fishing nations like Italy and Norway. There were others from the Mediterranean: Croatia, Greece, and even one from Algeria. There were other Scandinavians: Swedes and Finns; also Germans, Danes, and Russians. One fisherman came from Australia. There were U.S. citizens and Native Alaskans, too, but most came from overseas.

Many cards noted their immigration status: when they filed their first papers, or intent to naturalize, and second papers, the formal petition to become a citizen. At least one fisherman was reported held by immigration authorities. The cards don't list race but mention "complexion." Scandinavians tended to be labeled as "fair" or "light," while fishermen from the Mediterranean were usually listed as "dark." Some were described as "ruddy."

The cards list the canneries where the fishermen worked using APA's shorthand for the different canneries: such as the <NN> in South Naknek and the <NC> in Clarks Point. They listed the ships they sailed on: the three-masted barks of the APA's Star Fleet and the steamers that succeeded them in the 1920s. They recorded injuries: fractured ribs and injured hands. There were several cases of fish poisoning. It's often caused by eating raw or under-cooked salmon but can also come from handling fish. Several deaths were noted on the cards. The work was hard, the hours long, and the tides, winds, and weather were unforgiving. Overall, two or three fishermen died in Bristol Bay every year.

The company identified "trouble makers," probably union activists, and noted detentions and fines for insubordination. They listed other problems: one fisherman refused to sail on the Star of France, a Dillingham fisherman was caught trying to deliver old fish, and another was caught using small mesh gear. Fishermen then were paid by the fish, not the pound, so they padded their catch by adding sections of net with mesh under 4½ inches to catch more small fish.

Many filled out their cards for 20 seasons in Bristol Bay. The cards list both the individual fisherman's catch and the cannery average, in numbers of fish. This was before they weighed the catch but you can estimate poundage by multiplying the first number by an average weight for sockeye: 6 pounds. 20,000 reds are 120,000 pounds and there are several years when it topped 30,000 reds, or 180,000 pounds.

These fishermen fished from their sailboats by hand. No motors, hydraulic net rollers, or power reels. Just two guys in a wooden boat who pulled their nets in by hand and pitched each fish to the tally scow with a peugh. When the wind went slack, they used their oars. For them, the Bristol Bay season lasted five months, from May to September. It took a month to sail north, a month to set up the cannery, a month to fish, a month to load the pack and close the cannery down, and a month to sail back to San Francisco.

During the sailboat years, Bristol Bay fisherman averaged 120,000 to 140,000 pounds of sockeye every year, even more on the East side. These catches did not come from exceptional runs. Total harvests averaged about 15 million sockeye annually, and rarely topped 20 million..

There are reasons why catch rates were higher then. Fishing wasn't regulated. Bristol Bay was open 24/7 until 1924. They fished 200 fathoms of gear, not the 150 fathoms used today. There weren't any district lines. Enforcement was non-existent. Effort was also smaller. Back in the 20s and 30s there were usually only 800 to 1,200 gillnetters in Bristol Bay and maybe a few hundred setnets. Now there are almost 1,900 drift permits and 1,000 setnets.

One of these fishermen stood out. Gennaro Camporeale was born in Italy in 1893, came to America and lived in San Francisco, half a mile from Fisherman's Wharf. He was an Able-Bodied seaman and started fishing in Egegik in 1914, when he was 21. He filed for US citizenship in 1929. Camporeale fished from the APA's <E> cannery for 19 seasons.

He stands out because among the cards of fishermen who routinely landed 20,000 and 30,000 fish annually, Camporeale and his unknown partner landed over 40,000 fish in 1918 - 240,000 pounds. And in 1922, he landed 45,500 reds, or 270,000 pounds of salmon pulled onboard by his hands and pitched into the tally scow.

All combined, in 19 seasons Camporeale landed over half a million sockeye at Egegik, some 3 million pounds. He had his off-years but he caught 15% more salmon than the average Egegik fisherman, 25% more than on the Kvichak, 40% more than Naknek, and twice as many fish as on the Nushagak.

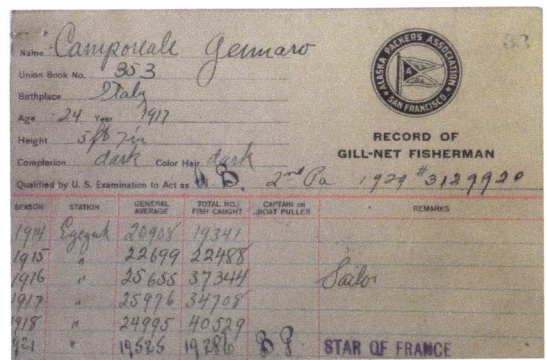

The APA cards don't record prices but contracts with the Alaska Fishermen's Union show in 1914 Bristol Bay fishermen were paid 3½ cents per fish, just over half a penny a pound. By 1937, the price was up to 12 cents a fish, two cents a pound. Add it all up, for the half million sockeye he caught, Camporeale earned a grand total of $18,000. Adjusted for inflation, that's almost $300,000 today, an average of $15,000 a season.

Camporeale was among the hardest-working highliners of the 1920s. For 19 years, he averaged about 170,000 pounds a year, fish pulled from Bristol Bay nets with his bare hands, and was paid an inflation-adjusted average of 19 cents a pound. Of course, the company paid for his boat, nets, and the Blazo in his Swede stove. The cannery also fed him and gave him a bunk during closed periods. Still, Camporeale amassed a remarkable record.

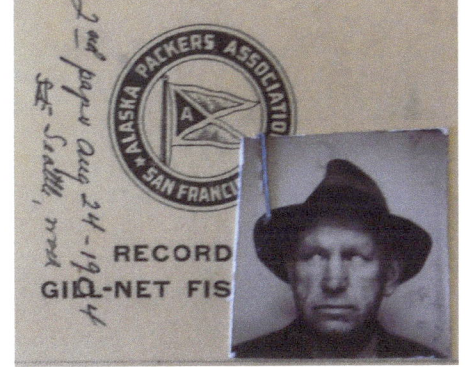

The APA kept photographs of some of the fishermen: blurry head shots stapled to the card, but maybe only of a few dozen out of the thousands of fishermen who worked during Bristol Bay's sailboat days. These are the faces of the iron men of Bristol Bay. There isn't a picture of Gennaro Camporeale, but each of these fishermen have stories too.

Fishing remains a tough business. Despite the power reels, hydraulics and electronic conveniences of today, it's still hard work. And it still can be deadly. But the sailboat days stand out as particularly tough and the men who fished during that time as exceptionally robust. If you walk through Bristol Bay's graveyards, you can find grave markers that include a small boat with a distinct sprit sail. They honor the men who fished during the sailboat days, and are counted among the Iron Men of Bristol Bay.

I was a cannery worker for nearly ten years, until the early 1930's. At this time Native people were allowed to fish, the kind of work we did normally at home. We also had become much more comfortable with English and Gasht'ana life in general. As fishermen we finally had the chance to make more money, and our life at Bristol Bay greatly improved.

PETE KOKTELASH

World War II saw a great change in Bristol Bay fisherman. Many of the Italians, Scandinavians and Finns were caught up in the military, or in wartime work and couldn't travel to Alaska to fish. Before the war the canneries didn't want to hire residents, but with the shortage of nonresident fishermen, they suddenly discovered that the Native Aleuts and Eskimos were marvelous boatmen and seemed to have been born to sail. Some of us resident whites didn't do so bad, either.

AL ANDREE

Nick Olympic from the Lake Iliamna region

The Struggle for Equity: Resident Participation in the Bristol Bay Commercial Fishery

By Tim Troll

The outside fishermen, immigrants from Italy, immigrants from other nations of the world, Norway, Finland, that came to this country were able to catch 2,000 fish a day when we were on limit, and us residents, if we were lucky, we were limited to 1,350. That went on until the 50's until we started raising a little bit of hell ourselves. Then we were also given second hand equipment by the great salmon industry . . . It still makes me mad to this day.

HARVEY SAMUELSEN

Alaska Natives were present in Bristol Bay thousands of years before the first cannery began operating in 1884. Yup'ik, Aleutiq and Athapascan people settled into the region for the very same reason the canneries did – salmon. Salmon was a resource so abundant and reliably present that it enabled these Native populations, unlike others in the arctic and subarctic, to give up a nomadic hunting life and build relatively settled communities.

As the salmon canning industry was gaining a foothold in Bristol Bay little thought was given to the welfare of the local Natives or the impact the industry had upon their culture and lifestyle. In 1884 when the first cannery began operating the Native people of the Bay had been exposed to western influence and goods for sixty-six years years. The Russians arrived in 1818 and built a modest fort and trading post at Nushagak, a mile or so below the village of Kanulik where that first cannery was built. Even though the impact of the Russians was profound, nothing in their previous experience prepared the local Native population for the changes that came with the salmon canning industry.

A salmon cannery is a huge industrial complex requiring many large buildings, a source of power and great quantities of water. In 1884 Bristol Bay was a vast wilderness of tundra, spruce, mountains and ice. Beyond the small trading post that remained at Nushagak after the sale of Alaska by Russia there was little western infrastructure to support the construction and operation of a cannery. All of the materials and men, including vast amounts of coal to power the cannery, had to be imported. The number of Non-natives who came to Bristol Bay to operate that first cannery in 1884 probably exceeded the total number of Non-natives that had ever visited the Bay since the Russians arrived. One can only imagine the awe and bewilderment of a local population living in small sod huts below the ground as they gazed upon the construction of such unimaginably large buildings and witnessed the constant flurry of human activity, the strange languages spoken and the incessantly loud and unfamiliar sound of steam engines and boilers.

During the formative years the negative impacts of the Bristol Bay commercial fishery outweighed the benefits to local Natives. Medical assistance was one benefit as cannery doctors extended help, but more often than not doctors were providing treatment for diseases like syphilis that became rampant after the canneries arrived. Cannery workers and fishermen also brought alcohol and opium and these drugs found their way into Native hands, often with disastrous results. Within a few years, however, a more paternalistic attitude developed as American missionaries arrived in the region. The Moravian church established a mission called Carmel near the first cannery in 1886. Within a few years canneries were providing some local employment and as early as 1887 Moravian Missionaries noted how large tent settlements of Natives started appearing around canneries. Some canneries also purchased fish from Natives and provided them with boats to use for set net fishing.

Most cannery efforts to provide for the local Natives were small tokens extended less out of a sense of responsibility than to placate Federal fishery managers who first appeared in the Bay in 1890. Despite the fact Native labor was often cheaper to obtain it was not enough to shift cannery employment practices. Imported workers and fishermen were preferred because they were captives for the season. Imported workers and fishermen were also protective of their employment and did not encourage the use of the local Natives. Canneries often claimed the Natives were unreliable because they were inclined to work only until they earned the small sums of money needed to purchase a winter's supply of the white man's goods they had come to depend upon – tea, flour, sugar, ammunition, cloth and the like. Not to be overlooked, however, was the fact that some cannery superintendents were simply prejudiced, a prejudice they were willing to set aside when extra labor was needed to process a large volume of fish. As the fishery completed its first decade in 1894 the Federal government was able to report that at three canneries on the Nushagak 468 persons were employed of which more than 25% were Native – an acceptable improvement. A Native fisherman in a cannery provided sailboat in the formative years was a rare sight, if seen at all.

The efforts of the Federal government to get more Natives and local residents employed in the canneries never really amounted to much more than a gentle prodding. Cannery interests were well entrenched in the halls of Congress. As a result Federal agencies charged with oversight of Alaska's fisheries rarely had budgets sufficient to take care of managing the fishery, much less taking care of Alaskans who wanted to participate in the industry. Even the elevation of Alaska to the status of territory in 1912 did little to help. Normally when Congress granted territorial status fisheries management was ceded to the new territorial government. Not so for Alaska. The canners feared an upstart territorial government and convinced Congress to retain federal control of Alaskan waters. Alaska's non-voting delegate was furious, but to no avail. The controversy, however, spurred a small but increasingly vocal opposition as Alaska residents began to resent industry dominance.

The independent fisherman was virtually non-existent in Bristol Bay. The canneries owned all of the sailboats and necessary gear and the unions representing fishermen, most of whom were non-residents, insisted on labor contract provisions that disfavored residents. The first local residents to actively participate as fishermen were probably individuals imported to Bristol Bay as fishermen who stayed behind after the season to take up residence as cannery watchmen or to prospect for gold. Many of these men married local women and eventually raised sons to be fishermen. A typical example would be "Glass Eyed" Billy Bartman, a seafaring Hollander who gave up that life to settle in Bristol Bay and raise a family. According to his daughter Helena (whose recollections are included in this book) her father

Peter Krause

Chris Peterson

taught her and her brothers how to fish from a sailboat. Robert Kallenberg, who came to Bristol Bay in 1928 as a teacher at Kulukuk recounted the first Natives he saw in a sailboat were Chris Peterson and Peter Krause. Peterson and Krause were sons of Euro-American fathers and Native mothers and were raised at the Moravian Mission at Carmel. Kallenberg himself lived in Bristol Bay for many decades, fished sailboats, served on the territorial board of fisheries and was a strong advocate for the rights of resident fishermen. During the 1920's and 30's approximately 1,200 cannery sailboats regularly fished Bristol Bay. However, as late as 1929 there were only 28 resident boats in all of Bristol Bay.

The experience level of residents grew as more fishermen made Bristol Bay home and passed their skills in sailboats along to friends and family. While Alaska could not provide all of the labor required to harvest Bristol Bay's salmon non-resident fishermen nevertheless increasingly felt insecure. Discord among resident fishermen grew as canneries adopted more discriminatory practices. Many of these practices were imposed upon canneries by virtue of collective bargaining agreements negotiated by the Alaska Fishermen's Union. Often resident fishermen were provided older boats and gear and were forced to wait while the boats of non-resident fishermen were allowed to deliver their fish. During peak runs swamped canneries would place resident boats on catch limits before non-resident boats. Canneries would sometimes pay higher prices to non-residents or did not allow residents to work for "run money" offloading and onloading ships at the beginning and end of each season. Perhaps the most over act of discrimination occurred when canneries required resident fishermen to paint an "A" on the side of their sailboats to identify them as Alaskan so the tally scows collecting fish could easily distinguish a resident from a non-resident.

The acrimony of Bristol Bay's resident fishermen reached a peak in 1939 as a result of two concessions the Alaska Fishermen's Union secured from the canneries. Canneries agreed to pay non-resident fishermen a bonus equal to one-third of all the money paid to residents for fish that residents caught in Bristol Bay. Also, non-residents were provided the first six boats for every caning line in Bristol Bay, virtually assuring them of employment through out the season, while resident fishermen might only be fishing during the peak of the run. The Alaska Territorial legislature attempted to address the plight of resident fishermen with the introduction of a bill in 1939 to require a hiring preference for residents in Alaska's fisheries. The bill passed the Territorial Senate unanimously, but failed for lack of one vote in the House. That failure provoked resident fishermen to seek help from Anthony Dimond, Alaska's delegate to Congress. The cause became even more urgent when the Federal Bureau of Fisheries announced that commercial fishing in Bristol Bay would be curtailed by 50% in 1940 to allow for greater escapement. Bristol Bay resident fishermen feared they would have no work at all. Dimond introduced legislation that would require that "all persons engaged in fishing in Bristol Bay in 1940 be residents of the territory." The bill failed to garner the necessary support.

Despite all of the efforts to make the Bristol Bay fishery more responsive to the needs of residents, parity was not achieved until it was virtually impossible for non-residents to participate - a condition that was created when the Japanese bombed Pearl Harbor and invaded the Aleutians.

The Second World War changed the landscape of the fishery. The labor traditionally employed by the canneries was drafted to fight or was needed in war industries. Cannery operators needed to draw upon resident labor. Cannery workers were not only needed, but more fishermen as well. During the war canneries were no longer reluctant or beholding to non-resident fishermen to put residents into sailboats. After the war there was a partial return to policies favoring non-residents, but the competence of Alaskans as fishermen and cannery workers was firmly established. As sailboats gave way to power boats Bristol Bay residents, both Native and Non-native, were at the forefront of a new era – the era of power and independent fishermen.

An experienced sailboat fisherman who wanted to fish one of these cannery-owned sailboats tossed his fish book to a cannery superintendent as proof of his ability. Invariably the super looked at the catch record toward the end of July. If the fisherman had missed that last week of delivery, he'd ask, "how come you didn't make any deliveries after July 20th? Were you up the Naknek River on a drunk?

The super didn't want fish on July 4th, which is when the run peaked. He had fish coming out of his ears then, and likely boats were on a limit. But late in the season he wanted every boat to bring in salmon daily, even if it was only 200 or 300 fish.

AL ANDREE

You had to use the tide because the tide was your master for sailing.

ALEC PETERSON

Sailboats were often towed to and from the fishing grounds.

A PEEK AT THE PAST
Helena (Bartman) Andree

I crewed in a Bristol Bay double-ender sail boat with my Dad in the mid 1930's. I was his only crew on the boat. In those days there was only room for a captain and one crew member.

My brother, who normally fished with Papa, got sick during the middle of the fishing season. Papa couldn't find a man to replace him so I was taken on as crew. In those days very few women, if any, went drift gillnet fishing in sail boats. At that time I was an eager teenager and proud to go as I knew that Papa was one of the most dependable and experienced boatman in Bristol Bay.

In those days the sailboat was the only water transportation used in Bristol Bay. Papa left his home in Rotterdam, Holland at the age of 14, hired on as cabin boy. He sailed around the world on freighters seven or eight times arriving in America in 1905 as a very experienced sailor. At the Port of San Francisco he met some Alaskan fishermen, who convinced him to go to Alaska and fish in the Bristol Bay fishery, where they used 30 ft. sail boats.

Not only did Papa become a fisherman but his career also included carrying freight, mail and passengers by dog team in Southwestern Alaska. Papa married a Yup'ik lady, my mother, and raised three sons and two daughters.

Papa taught each of us children how to mush dogs and sail.

I recall my fishing season with Papa in the mid-1930's – not a "push button" experience. Our anchor was thrown and pulled manually. We erected the sail, sprit and boom by hand. I remember hearing and enjoying the sail rings as they clickety-clacked up the mast. I learned the importance of the centerboard.

The foc'sle with a fitted tent was our kitchen and bunk room – which hardly had room enough for two large fishermen. Since Papa was only a very slight 5 ft. three inches, and I not much bigger, we made out just fine. A Swede stove was our cook stove and heated our tent.

We had no CB or radios to use in an emergency. A rain slicker on the end of an oar stuck up was the recognized distress signal. Our "john" in the stern, was a bucket with hunk of rope tied to the handle so we could empty it overboard and clean.

Our mattress was a reindeer skirt, which we rolled up when not in use and stowed in the bow of the sailboat along with our clothes and feather sleeping bag that Mom made. Papa, a true sailor, kept everything "ship shape" and we all learned how to keep order early. Anchor line and any other line had to be coiled appropriately, as well as any nets aboard.

We got ten cents a fish for our catch, which we had to deliver to tally scows where we then peughed the fish on board by hand. Peughs are illegal now, and modern fishermen use commercially made brailers to hold their fish, which are weighed and sold by the pound. We also had a bucket to bail water out of our boat. Some sailboats did have hand made bilge pumps.

The twelve foot oars were always handy, in case of an emergency. Commonly these were called "Scandinavian kickers." The oars were quite awkward and large for me to use, but Papa managed them quite well. We had to use the oars when there was no wind to sail, and used to assist our delivery of a large load of salmon to a tally scow. We used the oars also to help make turns. An oar was also used for a ridge pole to hold our tent, in the bow. Oars were also a fathometer. Our real fathometer was a 3/16 line with a 3 or 4 pound lead weight on the end. Our only navigational aid was a compass and Papa never left home without one.

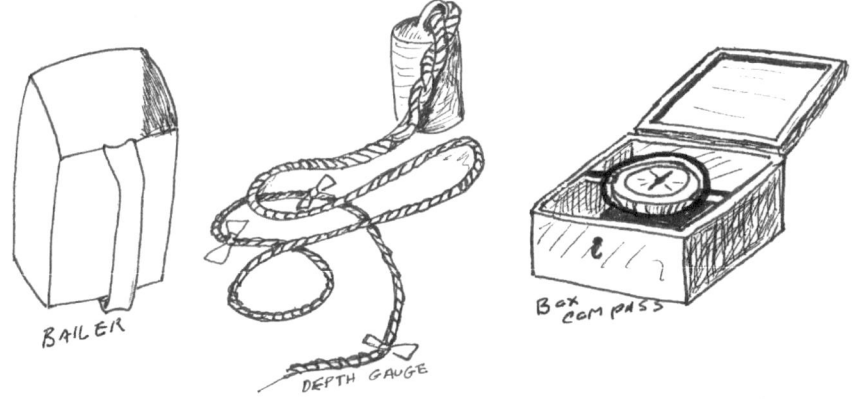

Helena (Bartman) Andree is the daughter of Dutch seaman "Glass-eyed" Billy Bartman a legendary dog team mail driver and fisherman who settled in Bristol Bay in the early 20th century

In those days fishermen respected each other; they'd let you drift before they set their net - to get out of the way. Oh a couple of guys they'd cork you, but most of the guys were gentleman. You were never trying to rush each other.

MARTIN "POYKEN" JOHNSON

The fisherman's trade was no game for a greenhorn. Every move had to count and immediate execution was necessary. The "skipper" was senior man in the boat. The "puller" was the deckhand with equally important duties. When the fishing boat approached a fish scow to unload, it was imperative that there be absolute unity between the two men as there was no margin for error. When the skipper dropped the sail and yelled "let her go," the puller had to throw the tie-up line at the instant the sail was lowered or the boat would be carried past the scow causing no end of delay and lost fishing time.

RAY PADDOCK

The Italians always had a stay from the top of the mast to keep the mast from falling back into the boat in case it broke, but the Scandinavians scorned this.

GUS DAGG

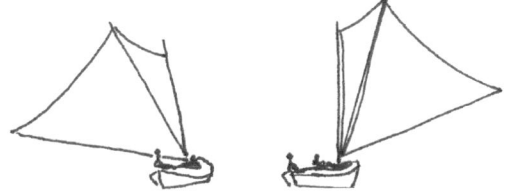

*A big storm could blow us off course.
A sudden strong wind could rip the sails.
In those days, clear skies and a strong
wind were welcomed by all fishermen.*

CHARLEY NELSON

You set your nets off the stern or sometimes off the bow. Then we got hand rollers. It made it easier on either side. You had roller cleats all over the boat on both sides. You could put the roller around to shift the weight. You would pull from the bow for a little bit and could use the wind and swells. You would pull with it, go ahead and pull again with the next swell. You could go ahead of it or on top of it, and you'd tangle the nets. You had to work all the time.

ALEC PETERSON

Whenever you decided what drift you were gonna make, night drifts in particular, you would make your set and that was it. You were committed for the drift. Usually pick up at low water, make another set and come back in with the flood.

ROBERT KALLENBERG

Carl Johnson standing in boat in the forground. Scandinavians pulled the net with the mast down. Italians, like those in the background worked with the mast up.

We pulla da net
to make da mon
to buya da bread
to getta strength
to pulla da net

Lament of the Italian fisherman

You'd get all the wealth of fish that you could. You'd shove them underneath the mast, in the cabin, everywhere.

ALEC PETERSON

Two well known stalwarts of the sailboat days "Hardworking Tom" Overwick (left) and Butch Smith (right) ca 1940. Overwick was an Icelander who sailed the world and came to Alaska as crew on a cannery ship. Smith came to Alaska during the Nome gold rush. Both adopted a lifestyle of prospecting in the fall, trapping during the winter and fishing in the summer. Observant local Natives who came to know Tom gave him the Yup'ik name "Nacayuilnguaq," which means "He never wears a hat."

A Sure 'Nuff High-Boat Fisherman

Comes a closed period and you and your boat puller party-up with a couple of cannery flappers in the old can loft. You get so pie-eyed you miss the tide the next morning while everybody else gets away to an early start to meet the fish out on the Big Sands. So what can you do - lay your net out in front of the cannery and doctor your hangover with a couple of hot rums while you wait for the tide to change?

You do just that and what happens? Your net starts smoking from float to boat as a school of reds starts smashing into the web, leaping, thrusting, churning in an orgy of self-destruction. In ten-minutes time you have to start hauling net, working like a madman to get it in before the fish drown and drag it to the bottom. Your arms feel as if you are wrenching them from their sockets, your back aches as you take the gear, cork by cork, over a roller that will not roll under such an overload, and your head ... Oh God, your head ... and your guts ... and your nerves. What a mess you are.

You get it in somehow. A swamping load. Fish in the clearing locker, in the side lockers, in the centerboard lockers, in the main fish bin, and even some up forward kicking and gasping in the bedding. You pick fish as if a pack of pitchfork devils prodded your rump, and you wind up peughing that load aboard the home tally scow and then go back to set out again and get another load before high water slack. Then you go through the whole back-breaking, soul-trying rigmarole once more.

The first thing you know another closed season rolls around and you stagger ashore too dead beat to even consider another party session in the can loft. That's when you find out that everyone else sailed past the fish when they went out. Up in the White House, the Superintendent is talking to the bookkeeper about you. "That son-of-a-bitch is a real fisherman," says the Brain. "Look how he spotted those fish while the rest of those bastards were sailing around like a bunch of Lake Union yacht clubbers." You are now a member of the elite . . . a sure 'nuff high-boat fisherman. It's as easy as that!

Truman Emberg, Dillingham, Alaska

I always stopped as skilled oarsmen passed; it was one of the most beautiful sights I've ever seen. Usually the captain or the tillerman steered the boat with the rudder and rowed with one oar, while his helper would push two oars.

AL ANDREE

One guy I fished with in Squaw Creek swamped me five times in one season. He got so hoggy. He couldn't control himself, he just kept pulling the net and pulling the net in even though the boat was sinking to the bottom. Luckily it was shallow. The monkey boat came and picked us up.

EARL "PAT" PATTERSON

THE FISHERMAN

Alaska, the land of romance –
Her tales are oft retold;
The grandeur of her mountain peaks;
Her valleys rich with gold.
The silver horde that comes and goes;
Of fortunes made in a day.
The romance of the miner-
As he mucks in the earth for his pay;
The romance of the musher,
As he hit the cold, cold trail –
Bleary eyed and frozen stiff
To get thru' the Dawson mail.

I've read her tales by the thousands
From Cape Nome to Ketchikan,
But never a poem or even an ode
About the Fisherman.

No weakling here can take a chance,
They're weeded out like chaff
No beardless youth or city dude
Can stand the hard, hard gaff.
Men with lots of guts, my lad –
Men that never cry
For they have to fight from dawn to night
Or else go down and die.

With a thirteen-foot oar
On that rough lee shore
You have to pull like sin-
The roaring waves will be your grave
If ever you give in.

You fight like hell with never a yell
To get in a fathom of net;
You've had no sleep and nothing to eat
And your clothes are wringing wet,
You've fished the sands, those treacherous sands
'Till your very soul is sick;
Your mouth's red hot and your eyes bloodshot –
But it's pick, you buggers, pick.

So here's to all the boys of the game –
Here's to the miner bold.
Here's to the musher of Arctic Trails
When they are icy cold.
And to the trapper and to the skinner,
For all of them have sand,
But the last and loudest cheer
We'll give to the **FISHERMAN**!

      Bill Wooten 1917, Fisherman
      Columbia River Packers Assn., Naknek, AK.

Alec Alvarez and Paul Chukan of Naknek delivering to talley scow, ca 1940

The way it worked was the boat would come alongside the scow. You would tie them up. There was a narrow walkway around the scow where you could stand. You had a tally machine the size of a large watch in your hand. As the fishermen peughed the fish you would punch the machine for every fish that went up into the air and into the scow. When you reached a hundred you would sing out "tally."

Sometimes they would come alongside to be tallied. You would ask them if they had any dog salmon. They'd say no. You'd tally them up for reds. But at night, by a coal lantern, the tallyman couldn't tell. Next morning you'd go out at daylight and there would be all these dogs in the scow.

AXEL WIDERSTROM

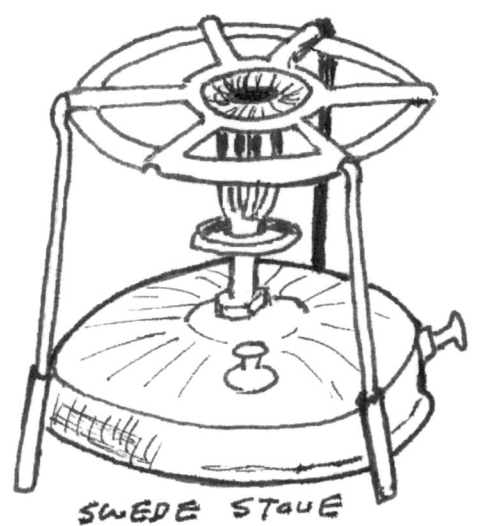

For heating and cooking purposes the sailboats had two different types of stoves, depending on the nationality of the fisherman. The Italians had coal stoves and the Nordics had a gas primed Swedish stove. It was easy to tell the different kinds of boats, because a Nordic boat would have a white sail and an Italian boat's sail would be dark from the smoke of the coal stoves. When it was dry weather you would have to be very careful with a coal stove because if a spark got on the sail, it would go up in flames.

ELMER "RED" HARROP

We had a little Swedish stove to cook on. You had to hang on to the coffee pot with one hand and the stove with the other - those boats would rock so hard.

SUERRE GJEMSO

In 1928, no Italian would be caught dead using a Swede stove and no squarehead would use what we called a dago stove. But toward the end of the sailboat era, a lot of guys from either side, including myself, used both. We found that the Italian stove was much better for heating and drying out the tent than the noisy, kerosene-smelling Swede stove, but the Swede stove was better for cooking.

GUS DAGG

I was first assigned to a boat operated by an old man named Hank. Hank and his regular partner Mike lived on the Alaska Peninsula. Hank and Mike were a breed that does not exist anymore. They were remittance men. Remittance men were usually incurable alcoholics, but Hank was not. He only got drunk twice a week, on Tuesday and Friday and was very proud of the fact that he never touched a drink on any other day. Mike was more or less drunk all the time. ...The mast fell down and hit Hank on the head the last day of fishing. He died happy. It was Friday, his day to get drunk.

GUS DAGG

Oh, there was whiskey. My brother was making whiskey on Ekuk Point. He had a container and a Swede stove, he had everything. Those old fellers, they sure liked their whiskey. They was a rugged bunch. But good-natured fellers. Drunk, but tough out on the water.

SUERRE GJEMSO

We were sailing in and got stuck on a sandbar outside of Libbyville. One of Alaska Packers tugboats was stuck out a little ways. A deck hand, his name was Andy, played one of those Swedish chromatic accordians with three rows of keys. He was playing all the Swedish music on the accordian and all these fishermen were out dancing all over the sandbar out there and the tide was coming in. Everyone was happy because it was the last day of the season.

EARL "PAT" PATTERSON

The worst thing that could happen to a gillnetter was to go aground at the height of a storm. The shoal water that is found throughout the bay has cost many a fisherman his life. The old-timers were an ingenious bunch and they figured out a ploy to prevent the surf from captizing the boat. Swiftly, the fishermen would strike the mast and lay it athwart ship. There they would lash it by passing lines under the hull and securing inboard. In this manner some sailors fashioned a "jerry-rigged" outrigger and were able to survive until the tide returned and floated the boat. If the boat turned over in the surf, the fishermen seldom survived the cold water and the silt dragged them down.

RAY PADDOCK

Pages from the photo album of
Alfred J. and Martha Opland

COURTESY ROBERT AND MILDRED OPLAND
PHOTOGRAPHS BY THOMAS G. PRATT CA 1930's

The First Load Of Cannery Workers To Arrive

Out Before 6:00 a. m. To Begin Drifting

The Tide Is Out And We're Still On The Beach

Calm Weather Makes A Tow Necessary - Early Morn

It Looks Good Today - We'll Get Out Early

Bristol Bay Fairly Bristles With Masts At Dawn

The Eve Of A Fishing Holiday - Towed In By A Scow

We Didn't Do Much Today But We'll Give Em Hell Tomorrow

The "Tally Man" Records The Salmon # 60

Red Salmon In The Boat - Dago Red In The Man

Pewing The Catch From A Well Loaded Fish Boat

By The Aid Of Ample Water The Scows Are Unloaded

The "IRON CHINK" Removing Salmon Heads

Trays Out Of The Retorts

Filled Cans Coming From The Lines To Fill Trays

Checking Weights Of Cans

Different companies had somewhat different styles of sailboats. Fisherman liked both the Nakeen and Carlisle Packing Company boats for they were narrow in the bow and fast under sail. Libby boats also had a sharp stern and a fairly sharp bow. Columbia River Packers boats, with a sharp bow and a sharp stern, were also among the best sailing boats. Red Salmon boats were also good sailers. Alaska Packers boats had a fat bow and a fat stern, and many fishermen referred to them as "barnacle boxes" and didn't think much of them as sailers. However, they were marvelous for packing a big load of fish. I've seen 3,000 fish that average close to six pounds each come out of a Packer's boat.

AL ANDREE

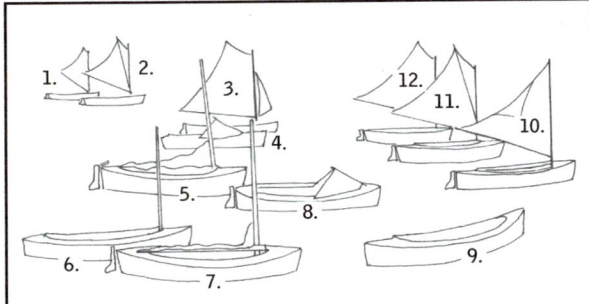

Bristol Bay double-ender colors near the end of the sailboat days

1. Alaska Packers Association (APA), Diamond J, Kvichak
2. Libby, McNeil & Libby, Libbyville
3. Red Salmon Canning Co., Naknek, Ugashik
4. Bristol Bay Packing Co., Hungry's Cannery, Pederson Point
5. Libby, McNeil and Libby, Graveyard Cannery, Koggiung
6. Alaska Packers Association (APA), Diamond NC, Clarks Point
7. Intercoastal Packing Co. (IPC), Naknek Point
8. Red Salmon Canning Co., Naknek, Ugashik
9. Pacific American Fisheries (PAF), Warren, Nornek (Naknek) and Dillingham
10. Great Atlantic and Pacific Tea Co. (A&P), Nakeen
11. Columbia River Packers Association (CRPA), Bumble Bee, South Naknek
12. Alaska Packers Association (APA), Diamond NN, Diamond O and Diamond M at Naknek, and Diamond E at Egegik

The End of the Sailboat Days
The Bloody Fifth of July, 1948
by Bob King

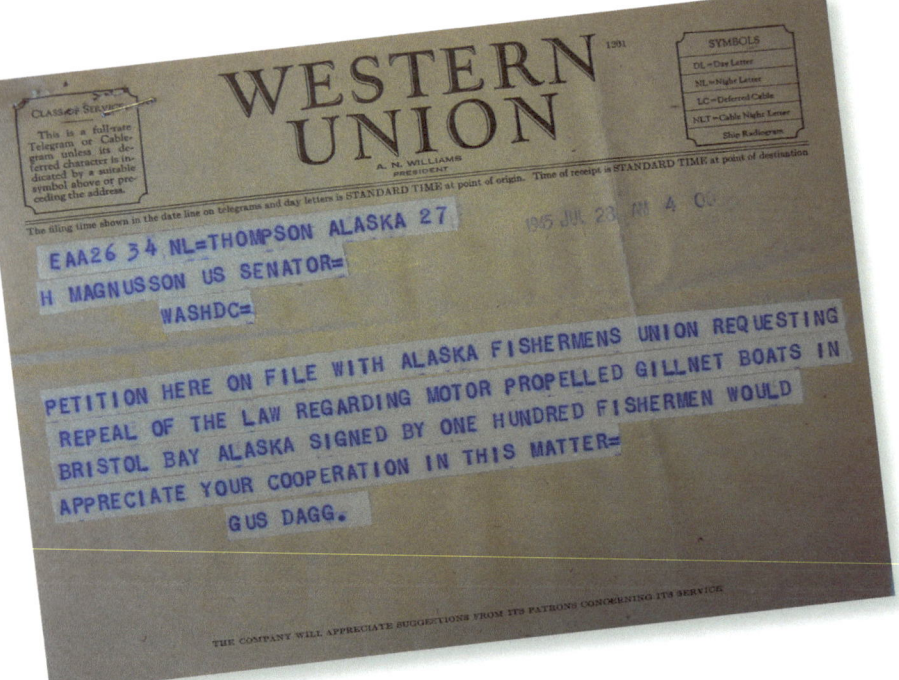

The end of World War II brought new technology that would soon change the canned salmon industry in Bristol Bay, but not without a final fight over that remnant of 19th century technology – the sailboat.

In 1946, the canning industry broke with its sea-going tradition and chartered Pan American Airways to fly fishermen and cannery crews to Bristol Bay, landing at the air base constructed at King Salmon during the build-up to the war. Chevron Oil started tanker service to Bristol Bay bringing gasoline and fuel oil to power canneries. Advertisements in Pacific Fisherman tempted fishermen with wartime electronics like radar and sonar converted to civil purposes. Meanwhile, fishermen in Bristol Bay still worked their nets from sailboats.

The war was still raging when fishermen petitioned the U.S. Fish and Wildlife Service to replace their sails with powerboats, commonly used elsewhere in Alaska. In a telegram from South Naknek on July 27, 1945, a week before the first atomic bomb was dropped, Gus Dagg of the Alaska Fishermens Union asked for help from freshman United States Senator Warren Magnuson.

Sailboats had been used in Bristol Bay since the fishery began in 1884 and powered boats were banned by law since 1924, supposedly to conserve the salmon runs. But as technology improved, fishery managers with the U.S. Fish and Wildlife Service began to have doubts about the rationale to keep sailboats. The increased use of power scows by canners in 1946 to haul fish back to their canneries drew the following observation in the Service's annual fishery report for Bristol Bay:

> *Motor propulsion helps the fishing operation in getting to and from the fishing grounds ... and not in the catching of fish. If such a trend (in power scow usage) continues it is evident that the prohibition against the use of power as a conservation measure will be largely, if not entirely, circumvented.*

Later that fall, members of Alaska Fishermen's Union voted 1,116 to 156 in favor of the use of powerboats in Bristol Bay. Union leader Hans Hansen bristled with wartime rhetoric:

If the Congress continues to countenance our being forced to continue fishing in outmoded sailboats, then it ought to start a movement back to the days of (the) horse and buggy. They ought to give the Army bows and arrows and the Navy dugout canoes instead of the billions they're getting now for the A-bomb.

The canning industry continued to insist that sailboats were needed as a conservation tool. "Any sudden relaxation of the rule prohibiting power will leave your Service with little or no control over the fishing effort," wrote E.E. Murray, chairman of a group of Bristol Bay cannery operators in a letter to the Fish and Wildlife Service. "The area is better adapted to the present method of fishing than any other and … the interests of conservation are best served by the use of a fishing unit, the efficiency and intensity of which is well known and understood by the Fish and Wildlife Service, cannery operators and fishermen alike."

Milt James, of the Fish and Wildlife Service, didn't buy it: *"Over the past 15 years the operators have done everything possible to minimize the importance of this measure in conserving the fishery … (the use of monkey boats and power scows to tow sailboats) have virtually nullified the prohibition on motor propelled fishing boats as a conservation measure."*

The conservation of fish was largely a cover, the industry had other concerns. Murray conceded the change to power would render the entire fleet of some 1,500 sailboats obsolete and require the investment of millions of dollars in new boats at a time when salmon runs were on the decline. The canners also had competitive worries. The post war period saw an increased use of ships that could freeze the salmon to be canned elsewhere that posed a threat to the established industry.

The Fish and Wildlife Service urged the canners and fishermen to work together to transition to power boats by the 1948 season. The canners balked and instead proposed restrictions on their use of power scows as a compromise. As the 1948 season got underway, two Dillingham fishermen took matters into their own hands. Frank Wood and Nels Hedlund bolted an outboard motor to the rudder of their sailboat. They were caught and became the first and only fishermen to be charged with a violation of the powerboat prohibition. The two pleaded guilty and their 10-horsepower Johnson outboard, valued at $125, was confiscated.

As the 1948 season progressed, it became one of the roughest in years with winds of 25 to 30 miles per hour and gusts up to 50 mph. On the 5th of July, during the peak of the salmon run, Stanley Johnson of the Alaska Fishermen's Union took a ride on a cannery tender to observe the fleet in action. It was a calm morning, but the weather was soon to change.

"We hailed boat after boat and they were really pulling them in. Anywhere from 1,600 to 2,000 fish already," Johnson later wrote. They offered two fishermen a tow back to the cannery while they picked their nets when the wind picked up. "It was really strong and rising fast. Everywhere you could see the boats were running for cover, with their sails snugged down." When he looked back at the boat under tow, he saw the men were in trouble. They were bailing like mad and taking on water, slipping and falling in the fish as they worked. I began to haul in on the line to bring them alongside, and just as I brought them in, over she went. Both men jumped, one making it to the deck and the other hanging over the side until he was pulled aboard. The boat and the fish, the work of a whole night and a half of day, was gone. The net fouled the tender's propeller and while they fought to cut the net loose, a fishing boat came roaring past. "There's a couple of guys who will make it safely," Johnson remembered thinking.

And then something happened that still gives me cold sweats sometimes. One of the guys in that boat, wearing yellow slicker, was a man I'd known for some time. The other was a Native whose name I didn't know. And their boat raced on by us, maybe 200 yards away and then flip! Up and over she went! All of us were frozen stiff at the (s)ight. The boat went clear out of sight, then came up out of the trough of a wave bottom side up with two men hanging onto the keel. Down she went again, out of sight, then up with both men still hanging on. Down out of sight again, then up … and the guy in the yellow slicker was gone. We never saw him again. It was really murder to have to stand there helpless and watch that guy go. We couldn't toss a line that far. We tried tossing a life ring but couldn't reach them.

Another power scow rescued the Native fisherman when the tender received a radio call about two fishermen hanging onto nothing but a sailboat mast out in the middle of the river. They couldn't reach the fishermen, but a monkey boat rammed into the sands nearby "and got his stern up against the two guys and got them aboard."

The day has come down in the lore of Bristol Bay as the "Bloody 5th of July" a description that suggests many fishermen drowned that day. However, press reports at the time indicate just one fisherman died, Olaf Koppen of San Francisco, about 55 years old. Five other fishermen did die that year. Gustav Olson, 56, of Seattle and Ole Lamvik, 63, of Portland drowned July 2; and Hjalmar Harju, 56, of Kalama, Washington, and Oscar Peterson, 27, of nearby Woodland were lost July 7, 1948. The sixth fisherman was not identified. Regardless of the number of deaths, the strong winds of 1948 created enough havoc among the hapless sailboats to impress the U.S. Geodetic Survey of the dangers of fishing in Bristol Bay. The Survey published a maritime chart of Kvichak Bay in 1949 based upon depth soundings made during that treacherous 1948 season. The Chart officially identified and named the shoals off Johnson Hill as Deadman Sands.

The six drownings in 1948 were cited by fishermen as examples of the risks they faced in sailboats, but the salmon canners remained firm and continued to dismiss charges that sailboats were unsafe. As for the deaths in 1948, the canners contended sleep and greed were the real causes:

Two of the fishermen who lost their lives during the 1948 season were run down on a dark night while asleep in their boat. The absence of power could not have contributed to the accident. The other four lost their lives because unusually severe storms arose suddenly during peak periods of the run when their boats were overloaded.

Meanwhile, the canners by their own actions began to undermine their argument that sailboats were a conservation tool. During the 1949 season two canneries effectively worked around the power restriction by using power scows and monkey boats to transfer sailboats between fishing districts to gain greater access to fish. The Fish and Wildlife Service noted both the irony and brazen nature of the practice:

Two operators from the Naknek immediately broke all previous precedent ... by towing their boats down into the Egegik District and receiving fish on their power scows. The efficiency of this operation can be directly attributed to monkey boats and power scows. It was agreed later in the season that this practice would be discontinued, however, the fact remains that from the standpoint of mobility, we already have power.

Others joined in the call for change. The Territorial Legislature created the Alaska Fisheries Board in 1949. One of its first actions was to say the regulation against powerboats in Bristol Bay could no longer be justified on conservation grounds. "The safety of fishermen has been entirely overlooked," said board chairman Clarence "Andy" Anderson. With fishermen, the territorial fish board, and its own biologists pushing for change, the federal government in late 1949 finally proposed abolishing the powerboat restriction beginning with the 1951 season.

"It has been contended...that the conservation of the salmon runs would be threatened by such a technological advancement," said Interior Secretary Oscar L. Chapman. "However, the Fish and Wildlife Service now possesses sufficient enforcement facilities and scientific knowledge to protect the runs against undue depletion despite the type of motive power utilized in the fishing boats."

The decision took the canning industry by surprise. "We are greatly disappointed by this sudden, unannounced change of policy," said Stan Tarrant of Pacific American Fisheries (PAF):

If the action ... authorizing power boats is designed to benefit Alaska and the residents, it is not only ill conceived, but it establishes a more efficient means of fishing...at a time when the runs of three out of every five years are in a declining state of productivity.

The Fish and Wildlife Service initially postponed implementation of the new law for a year to give the canners time to motorize its fleet. However, rather than accept the change, the canners made a last ditch stand to hold onto the sailboat. They appealed to resident fishermen to reject powerboats. W.C. Arnold of the trade association Alaska Salmon Industry, Inc. (ASI) sent a telegram to Elmer Harris in Naknek that said allowing powerboats into Bristol Bay would be a tragic mistake. In addition to the conservation concerns, Arnold argued that powerboats were unsafe and prone to mechanical breakdowns.

In the Dillingham Beacon, Wilbur Church retorted, "The industry apparently has not made up its mind whether the power boat is so efficient that it catches all the fish … or so inefficient that it spends its time drifting helpless while the fish go by."

Arnold upped the ante, claiming that allowing powerboats would invite fishermen from Kodiak and Cordova to rush into Bristol Bay and cause "quick economic death for the Dillingham area and severe financial losses and ultimate disaster for the rest of the watershed." In Naknek, Wards Cove Packing president Alex Brindle said a fleet of 500 tuna clippers was waiting to move into the Bay. "The proposal to permit power will completely eliminate salmon canneries on Bristol Bay as they now exist," Brindle asserted, and the result would be "the loss of over a thousand local jobs".

Wilbur Church saw these claims by the canners as an explicit threat to resident fishermen and fired back. "Obviously they have decided that if we don't agree with them in their fight against power, they won't buy any resident's fish … (and) plan to recruit more boats to continue their policy of favoring the non-resident."

In 1950, ASI sponsored a last-ditch petition drive to ban powerboats but drew resistance from resident fishermen. Press reports noted fistfights over the petition broke out in Naknek and union leader Jim Downey dismissed the signers of the petition in Dillingham as "setnetters, waitresses and deckhands" who were subject to "intimidation, bribery (and) misrepresentation."

The Fish and Wildlife Service held a final series of hearings on the powerboat question in late 1950 but there was little new added to the debate. To one fisherman, the question had nothing to do with conservation or any of the other common arguments against powerboats. Al Andree of Dillingham observed that it was simply a matter of money. "Sailboat fish is cheap. That is why the industry does not want to change," Andree testified. Powerboats would "give (fishermen) more bargaining power against the canneries." The canning industry stuck to its claim that sailboats were needed as a conservation measure. PAF's Stan Tarrant predicted, "if … the (Fish and Wildlife) Service permits the use of power it takes the responsibility for risking destruction of the most valuable single fishery in the world."

Federal officials shrugged off these last-minute intimidations. "From the point of conservation, the prohibition of powered gillnet boats cannot be justified or supported." The canners petition was rejected, Secretary Chapman's earlier order stood, and powerboats limited to 32 feet in length were allowed in Bristol Bay beginning with the 1951 season. The length limit on the new powerboats was first proposed in 1947 and was intended to "have the effect of restricting the intensity of fishing in the area to approximately the level of recent years."

Because the canning industry focused on preserving the sailboat rather than motorizing their fleets, only 86 powerboats operated in 1951. Boat builders soon mass-produced a fleet of new Bristol Bay powerboats. Bryant's Marina in Seattle offered a popular design with a 95-horsepower Chris-Craft gasoline engine and a hydraulic power roller to pull nets aboard. Bryant's gillnetters were utilitarian workboats but offered fishermen a covered pilothouse and cabin for $7,500. When the 1952 fishing season began eighty percent of the fleet, 895 vessels, were under power. The remaining sailboats were soon either converted to power or left to rot. By 1954 only 15 sailboats were still listed as active. They were the last sailboats to commercially fish in Bristol Bay.

Photo from William Paul Jr. photo collection, courtesy Ben Paul

Sailboats from Alaska Packers Assn. Diamond J cannery headed in for the closed period 1949. Photo by Mel Monsen, Sr. courtesy Mel Monsen, Jr.

Alaska Packers Association Diamond NN cannery at South Naknek. Photos from pages 70 to 77 were taken by professor Ole Mathisen (1919-2007) of University of Washington and University of Alaska, Fairbanks. Courtesy of his daughter Heidi Mathisen.

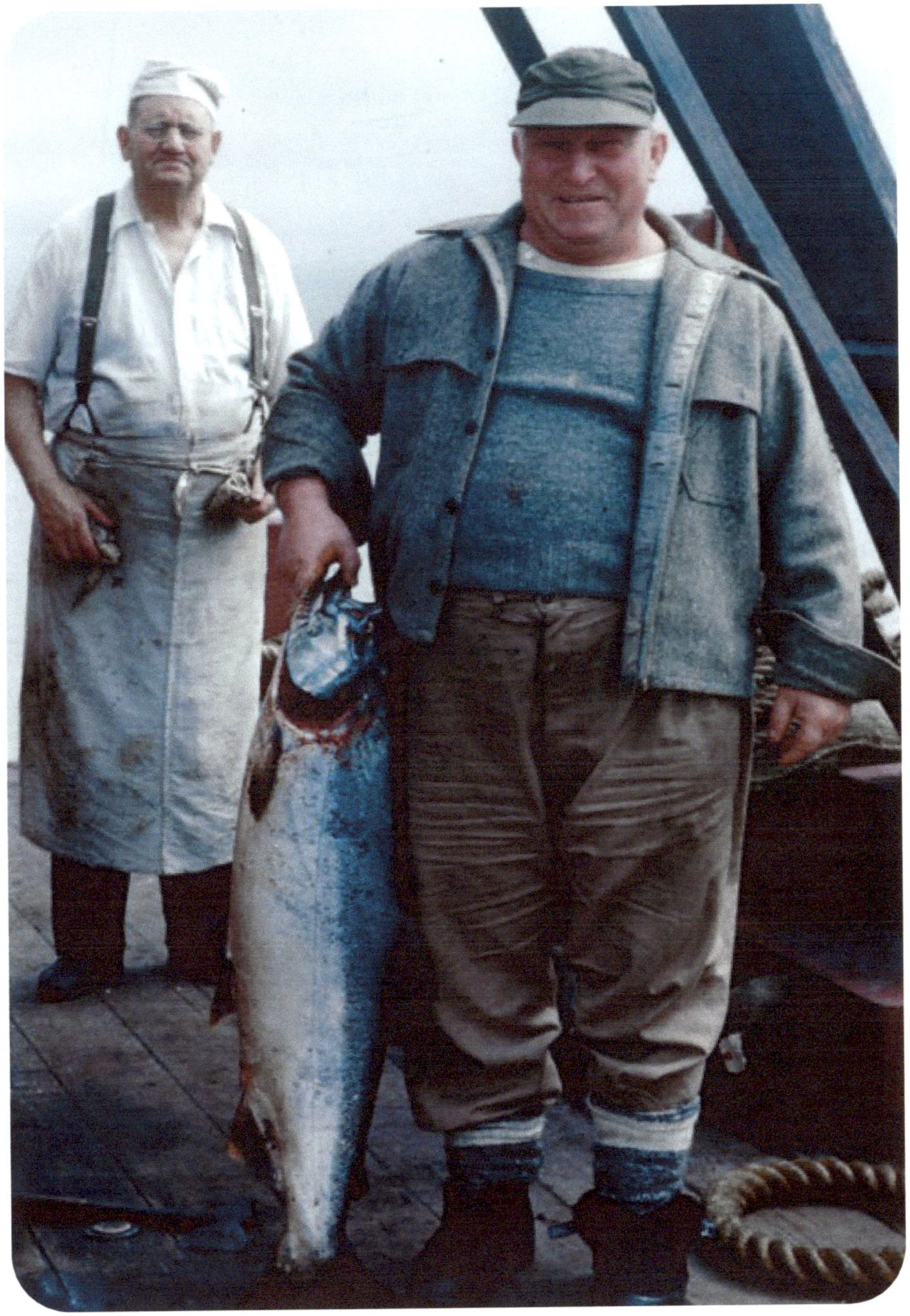

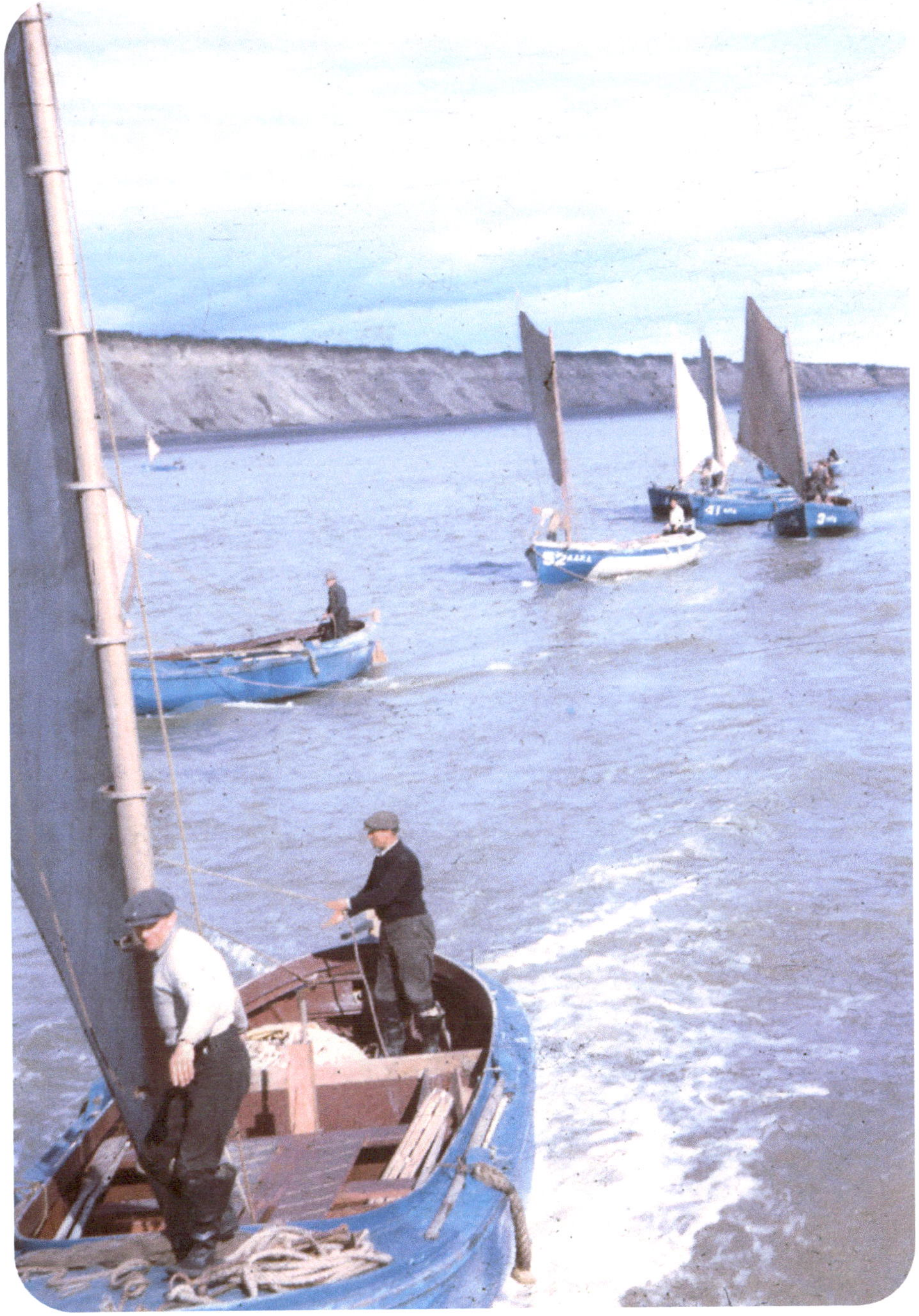

Converted sailboat *circa* 1952

New Bryant power boat *Rosalyn* among sailboat conversions at Pacific Alaska Seafoods dock in Dillingham *circa* 1952

With power boats the range was altogether different because you weren't at the mercy of the tides and particularly the lack of wind. You could be far more mobile. At the same time communications began to pick up. In the last of the sailboat days many of the sailboats had radio receivers and they would listen to the talk between the superintendents and the receiving stations and get some news as to where the fish were and gossip like that. But there was no two way communication and no communication between the boats. When two way radio communications set in with the boats that was what changed the picture again. Because they could talk with each other and friends would tell friends usually by some kind of code or other where they were. But anytime you saw several boats of one company pick up and head in one direction you'd be pretty sure that they were tipped off and everybody else would pull in their gear and take off after 'em, and so what little dabs of fish there were had far more intensive fishing pressure than they ever had during the sailboat days.

ROBERT KALLENBERG

Number of Boats Fishing	Year	Power	Sail
	1951	86	631
	1952	895	223
	1953	1108	62

New Bryant power boat belonging to Chief Ivan Blunka of New Stuyahok at Pacific Alaska Fisheries cannery dock, Dillingham, ca 1955.

I look back on the sailboats as foolish, hateful and dangerous, romantic and beautiful. Nothing will ever compare with the lovely sight of those great-winged graceful boats scudding with the wind across Bristol Bay.

AL ANDREE

In the sailboat days, the professional, year-round fisherman was an expert and far superior to the modern "part-timer." The present day school-teaching, moonlighting, gadget-depending, garage-mechanic type of fisherman did not appear until the sailboats were eliminated in the early 1950's.

GUS DAGG

The reason I was against power boats was because every Tom, Dick and Harry might fish. After legalization of power and the establishment of Limited Entry it seems there are now twice as many fishermen. These include doctors, lawyers and other professionals; it seemed all the pencil pushers started fishing. During sailboat days, they wouldn't have been able to fish, because they might have been afraid to sail. The rigors of sailing and living in an open boat would have been overwhelming.

JOHN NICHOLSON

Statement of the Territorial Board of Fisheries in 1950 on the Protection of Alaska's Salmon Fisheries

In studying the history of the decline of the salmon runs of the Pacific Coast, it is striking to notice how invariably these declines are blamed on over-fishing. These statements come most often from those least acquainted with the subject and are frequently made to cover up other causes, which may be of their own making.

While it is true that over-fishing is responsible for many declines, there is evidence to show that in numerous cases it is of minor or no consequence. The actual reasons are often found to be changes in the environment of the salmon due to natural and unnatural (man-made) conditions. This is especially true of the fresh water stages of its existence. Many examples could be cited. Some of the natural ones are cyclic climatic changes, floods, droughts, freezes, earthquakes, earth slides, beaver dams and increase in predators. On the other hand there are such man-made, or unnatural, causes as deforestation due to logging; hydro-electric, irrigation, flood control, and navigation projects; pollution, especially from pulp mills; soil conservation and reclamation schemes; gravel washing and mining operations; road construction such as stream culverts; insect control using poisonous sprays; and many others. The listing of these does not necessarily mean that all are inimical to the continuation of our salmon fisheries. It does mean, however, that if such projects are improperly and unwisely planned, the results will be disastrous to our fisheries. Alaska needs new industries, but not at the expense of her most important resource, which if properly cared for, will produce year after year.

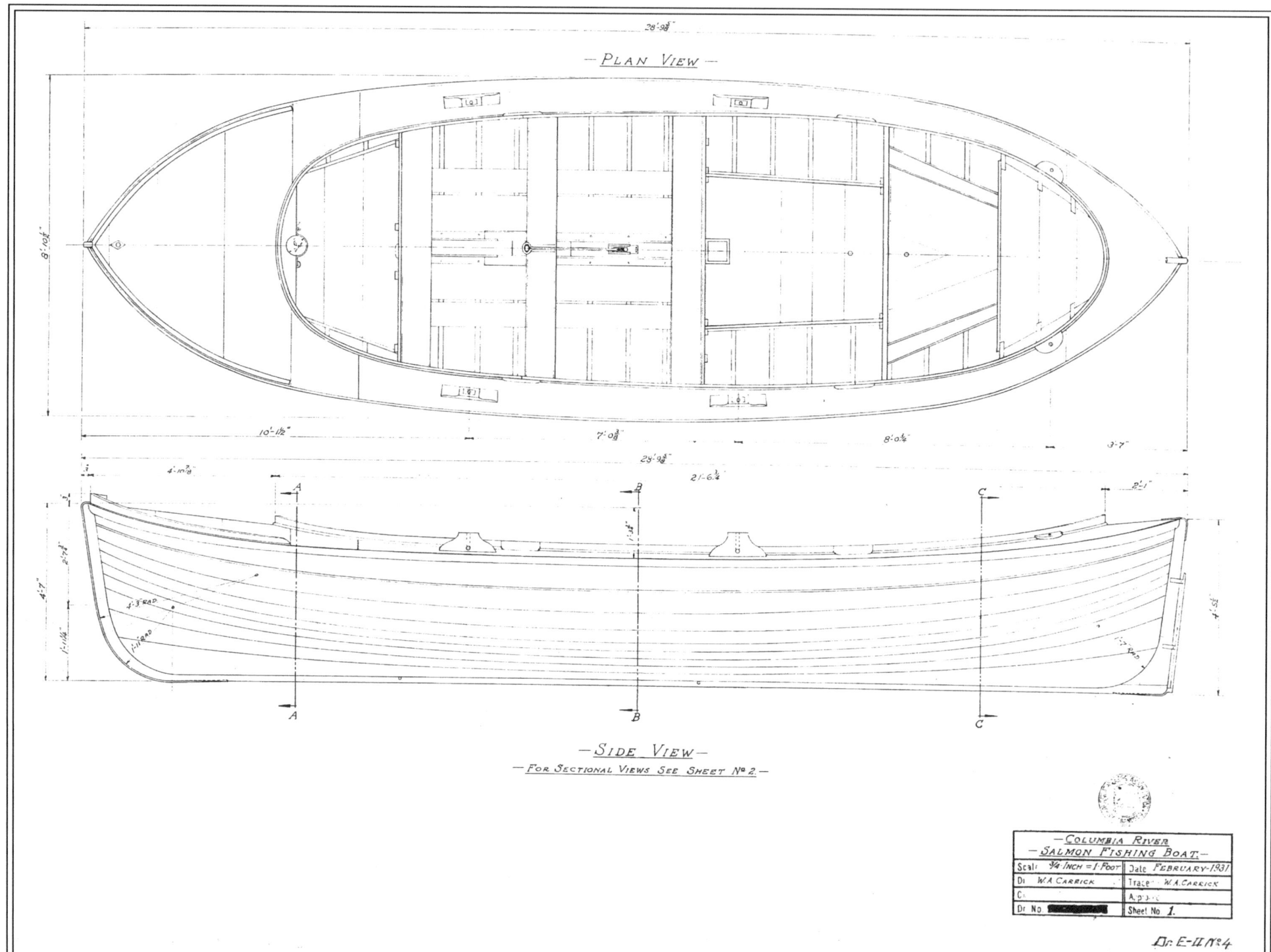

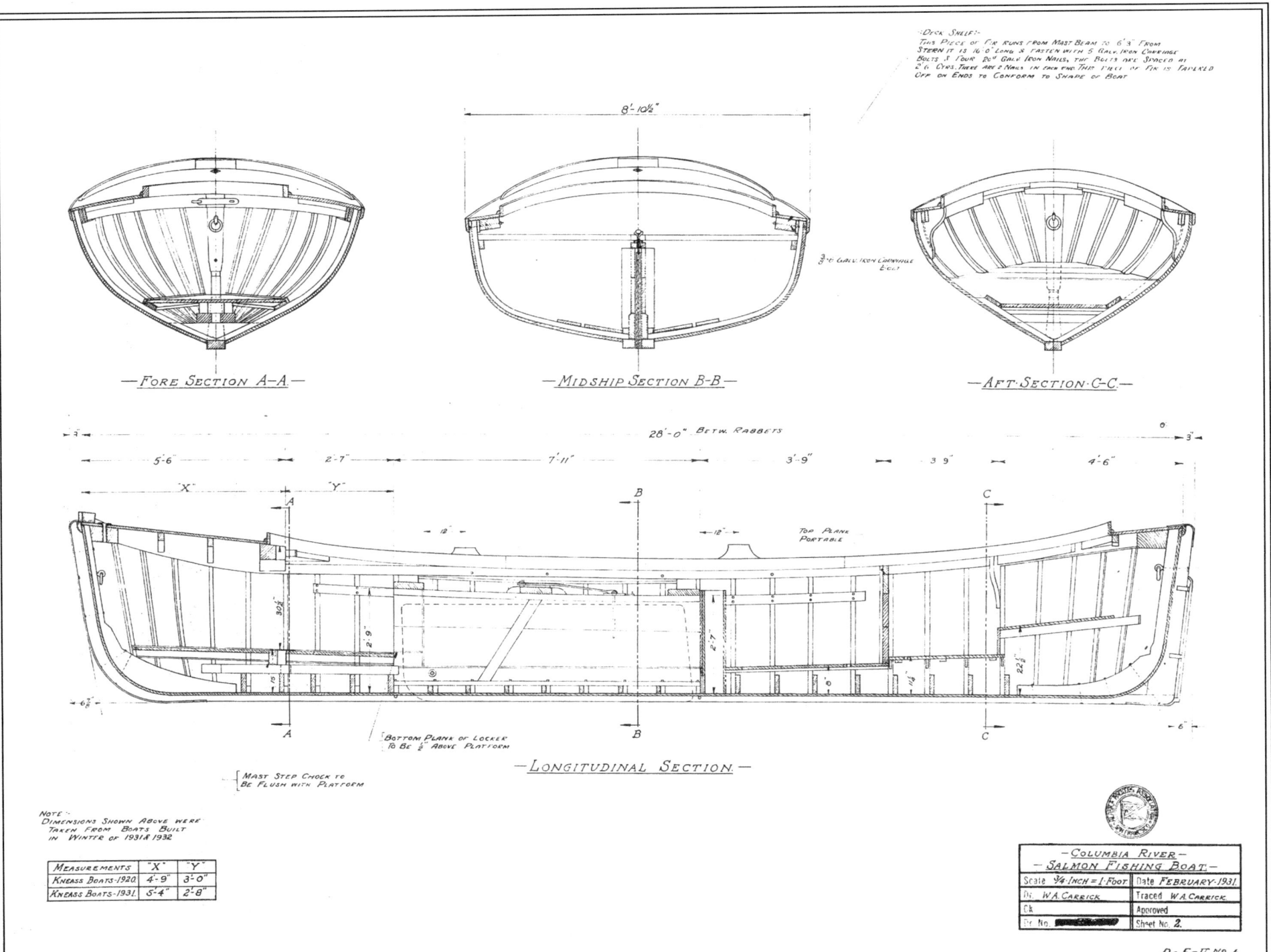

Mission of the Bristol Bay Heritage Land Trust

LAND PROTECTION: Purchases important habitat and subsistence value properties or protects them forever with non-development conservation easements (more than 30,000 acres protected)

SCIENCE: Funds research that enables us to focus our conservation efforts through a better understanding of the natural environment in Bristol Bay;

WATER PROTECTION: Secures water reservation and anadromous stream safeguards under Alaska law for salmon and all freshwater fish species of Bristol Bay;

ADVOCACY: Advocates for laws and regulations that protect the fish, wildlife and other renewable resources of Bristol Bay;

HERITAGE: Promotes awareness of the deep historical and cultural roots that bind people to Bristol Bay and its salmon resource;

EDUCATION: Provides the foundation for programs like the Bristol Fly Fishing & Guide Academy that engages the youth of Bristol Bay in conservation and employment opportunities tied to a healthy environment.

Your purchase of this book supports the Bristol Bay Heritage Land Trust. To find out more visit: www.bristolbaylandtrust.org

Credits, Sources and Historical Notes

Inset, San Francisco Maritime National Historical Park, Harry Hoyer Collection G11.23304n (hereafter Hoyer). Sailboats of the Diamond NN cannery on the beach at South Naknek.

Introduction. Hand tinted photo by Louis Gjosund Sr. courtesy Louis Gjosund Jr., Libby, McNeill and Libby cannery sailboat, Egegik ca.1935. All quotes from Axel Widerstrom taken from an unpublished manuscript entitled *Axel Widerstrom's Book of the Alaska Packers: as told to Karl Kortum*, San Francisco Maritime National Historical Park, Axel Widerstrom Estate Collection, HDC 565.

Opposite Page 1. Sailing off Flounder Flats, Nushagak Bay circa 1935, Photo by Dave Carlson, Dave and Mary Carlson Collection, Samuel K. Fox Museum, Dillingham. The letter "A" painted on the side of the boat at the stern identifies the boat as manned by fishermen who are residents of Alaska. For a period of time canneries distinguished resident fishermen from non-resident fishermen because privileges like higher prices, better sailboats or delivery preferences were extended to non-resident fishermen. Often this discrimination was required by the fisherman's union in the labor contract with a cannery. Most fishermen in the 1930s were non-residents.

Page 1 Photograph of Robin Samuelsen © Clark James Mishler. Photo of John W. Clark courtesy Elizabeth Nicholsen Butrovich.

Page 2. Map © Tim Troll

Page 3. The cannery at Kanulik (often called Rholff's cannery) was short lived. The Nushagak River was changing course and silt accumulation at the site (now named Rohlffs slough) probably made continued operation impractical. The cannery closed around 1905 and its equipment transferred to the Diamond NC cannery at Clarks Point.

Page 4 – 5. John N. Cobb – Alaska Packers Assn. Diamond NC Cannery, Clarks Point. 1918. University of Washington Library, Special Collections, John Cobb Collection COB216 negatives 4294-1, 4294-2 and 4294-3. (hereafter Cobb)

Page 6. San Francisco Maritime National Historical Park, John Olmi Collection P.83-034a

Page 7. Photo courtesy of Samuel K. Fox Museum, Dillingham, AK.

Page 10. Fishermen of Alaska Portland Packers Assn. circa 1907. (photographer unknown). "Run money" was the compensation paid to fishermen for work aboard the cannery ships during the month-long sail to and from Bristol Bay.

Page 11. Photo: Hoyer G12.6496n. New sailboats on beach at Northwest Fisheries Co. cannery at Nushagak ca 1910. Quote: Jefferson F. Moser, *The Salmon and Salmon Fisheries of Alaska: Report of the Alaska Salmon Investigations of the United States Fish Commission Steamer Albatross in 1900 and 1901.* (Washington DC: Government Printing Office 1902)

Page 12. Photo: Columbia River Maritime Museum, Astoria, OR. CRMM-CRPA 0574. Quote from Mel Hjorten taken from Martin and Tetlow, Flight of the Bumble Bee, *The Chinook Observer 2011*, page 163.

Page 13 Both photos by John E. Thwaites, circa 1906 Thwaites was a mail clerk on the S.S. Dora. P18-118, Alaska State Library, Thwaites Collection (top), Sailboats off Clarks Point, Nushagak Bay. University of Washington Library, Special Collection, PH Collection 247.393 (bottom). Sailboat with a rarely seen jib sail deployed. Italian fishermen sometimes used the jib sail.

Page 14. All quotes from Al Andree taken from *I Sailed or Salmon in Bristol Bay: Al Andree as told to Jim Rearden*, Alaska Magazine, July, August 1986; Reprinted in John Branson and Tim Troll eds. *Our Story: Readings from Southwest Alaska*, (Alaska Natural History Association, 2006) pp 180 –190. Photo: Cobb - Sailboats of the P.H.J. "Scandinavian" Cannery looking East to the Alaska Portland Packers Cannery, Snag Point (Dillingham) 1917. COB127. The Scandinavian cannery was built in 1885, the second in Bristol Bay. Local Yup'ik Eskimo people called the cannery workers at this cannery the *Atanvagmiut* meaning "the people with a big boss" (i.e. the cannery superintendent). This cannery ceased operating around 1955. The cannery in the distance is still operating as the Peter Pan Cannery. The cannery has processed salmon every year since it was built in 1901, a record allegedly unequalled by any other cannery in Alaska.

Page 15. © Clark James Mishler. Photo of Sailboats on the beach at Nushagak 1917. COB150

Page 16. Photo of Scandinavian fisherman by Sue Brown French courtesy of Dr. Charles Black and family.

Page 17. Photo by Al Andree, Helena Andree Collection 1997-48-40, Pratt Museum, Homer, AK. (hereafter Andree) According to Al Andree a year after this photo was taken Ralph Angilesco died from blood poisoning after he accidently struck himself in the wrist with a fish pick.

Pages 18 and 19. Photos in essay from the collection of the Alaska Packers Assn. at the archives of Western Washington University, Bellingham, WA.

Page 20. Photo: Cobb – Natives at Diamond N.C. Cannery, Clarks Point, circa 1917. COB214. All quotes from Peter Kokletash taken from *Dena'ina Perspective: Memories of a Bristol Bay Fisherman, Nuwendaltin Quht'ana: The People of Nondalton*, Ch. 11. Linda J. Ellanna and Andrew Balluta, Smithsonian Institution Press 1992.

Page 21. Andree 1997-48-3

Page 22. Guy F. Cameron, circa 1900, Anchorage Museum AMRC b02-1-1397.

Page 23. John E. Thwaites, University of Washington, Special Collections #247-0379.

Page 24. Photograph of Peter Krause by Dr. Linus H. French circa 1917 courtesy of Dr. Charles Black and family; Photograph of Chris Petersen circa 1934 by Ken Stevenson a former teacher in Togiak, collection of Samuel K. Fox Museum, Dillingham, AK.

Page 26. Hoyer G11.3059n. Great Atlantic and Pacific Tea Company (A&P) cannery at Nakeen, Kvichak River circa 1920s.

Pages 26 and 27. Anchorage Museum, Lu Liston 204, Snag Point (Dillingham) circa 1942. During World War 2 many canneries combined operations. This photo features boats from Red Salmon, Libby's Nakeen, A&P and PAF canneries. All quotes from Alec Peterson taken from: The Tide Was Your Master for Sailing, Uutuqtwa, Bristol Bay High School, Naknek, AK. Vol. 7, No. 1 (1982).

Page 28. Photo Ward Wells circa 1946, Ward Wells Collection, Anchorage Museum 83.91S0159-R01. (hereafter Wells).

Page 29. Photos: Andree 1997-48-13 (top); The A&P tug Nakeen and the power scow Teddy shuttling boats to the fishing grounds circa 1938. Anchorage Museum at Rasmuson Center, Lu Liston 1391.8. (bottom)

Page 31. Photo: John Olmi Collection P78-026a, San Francisco Maritime National Historical Park. Quote from Martin Johnson taken from film *Windfall Fishing Sailboats of Bristol Bay* produced by the Lake Clark National Park & Preserve.

Page 32. All Quotes from Ray Paddock taken from Robert Parrish, *Of Wooden Boats & Iron Men*, Alaska Fish and Game Magazine, May-June 1986. Ray Paddock a Tlingit from Tenakee Springs, AK began fishing in Bristol Bay in 1940. He was a pioneer of "Fishing to the Westward" for other Alaska Natives from Southeast, AK who followed in his footsteps to fish in Bristol Bay. See also, Robert Parrish, *Golden Years, Williwaws and Waves: Ray Paddock Marks 50th Year of Gillnetting in Bristol Bay*, Alaska Fish and Game Magazine, January-February, 1990.

Page 33. Andree 1997-48-29

Page 34. Andree 1997-48-15

Page 35. Andree 1997-48-21

Page 37. All quotes from Robert Kallenberg taken from an unpublished transcript of an interview with Mike Davis, March 12, 1995. Photo: Wells 83.910156-R0. Sailboat from Columbia River Packers Association below Diamond M cannery on the Naknek River circa 1946.

Page 38 San Francisco Maritime National Historical Park, John Johansen Collection, G.6.7.879. circa 1920. Carl Johnson, standing in the boat pushing off with oar fished for "Whitehead Pete" Nelson who had a saltery off Squaw Creek on Kvichak Bay.

Page 39. Lament quoted in Andrews and Larssen, Fish and Ships, Superior Publishing, Seattle, Washington, 1959

Page 40. Andree 1997-48-30. Photo of Smith and Overwick, Dave and Mary Carlson collection, Sam Fox Museum, Dillingham, AK (photographer unknown).

Page 41. Photo by Louis Gjosund, Sr. of his partner and brother Ed Gjosund when they fished for Libby, McNeil and Libby at its Ekuk Cannery on Nushagak Bay in the 1940s. Photo courtesy Louis Gjosund, Jr.

Page 42. Story by Truman Emberg from his book *Frolic Welcome* published posthumously by his wife Maxime in 1985. Truman was an outspoken advocate for Bristol Bay fishermen. He was elected to represent the region as its delegate to the Alaska Constitutional Convention in 1955.

Page 43. Hoyer G7.19.941n. All quotes from Earl "Pat" Patterson taken from Beverly Patterson, Earl "Pat" Patterson Uutuqtwa, Bristol Bay High School, Naknek, AK. Vol. 12, No. 2 (1989).

Page 44. Bill Wooten fished for Columbia River Packers Assn. His poem appeared in the January 1917 edition of *Pacific Fisherman* magazine at page 20

Page 45. Hoyer G11.2.503n

Page 46. Wells 156-R14. Paul Chukan and Alec Alvarez of Naknek delivering to tally scow, circa 1946.

Page 48. All quotes from Elmer "Red" Harrop taken from Mel Coghill Slime Time Uutuqtwa, Bristol Bay High School, Naknek, AK. All quotes from Gus Dagg taken from *Gus Dagg, Bristol Bay Sailboat Salmon Fishing, 1928, The Fisherman's News*, September 1975, Second Issue.

Page 49. Fishermen rafted up waiting for high tide circa 1920's. Photo shows the tent provided fishermen that was set up in the bow to provide some reprieve from the usually wet weather of the Bay. In this period fishermen often used leather hip boots (called Finn boots) softened with linseed oil or Kingfisher and Blue Ribbon brand rubber hip boots. Hoyer G12.30,264n

Pages 50 and 51. © Clark James Mishler, 2007

Pages 52 and 53. Thomas G. Pratt. From the photo album of Alfred J. and Martha Opland, courtesy Robert and Mildred Opland.

Page 54. Photo © Clark James Mishler, 2007. Wooden memorial in Dillingham AK graveyard.

Page 61. Illustration © Tim Troll. Information on sailboat colors provided by Melvin Monson Sr., Hjalmar (Ofi) Olsen and John Branson.

Page 62. Hoyer P78-026a (2)p

Page 63. Photo © Clark James Mishler, 2007

Page 68. Photo from William Paul Jr. photo collection, courtesy Ben Paul

Page 69. Photo by Mel Monsen, Sr. courtesy Mel Monsen, Jr.

Page 70. Photos from pages 70 to 77 were taken by professor Ole Mathisen (1919-2007) of University of Washington and University of Alaska, Fairbanks. Courtesy of his daughter Heidi Mathisen.

Page 79. Steve McCutcheon 1955, Anchorage Museum at Rasmuson Center, McMutcheon Collection, 26733. "Natalia" – a new Bryant power gillnetter belonging to Chief Ivan Blunka of New Stuyahok alongside the dock of the Pacific American Fishery (PAF) cannery at Dillingham in 1955. The designation on the side of the Natalia – NI – indicates Chief Blunka was a Nushagak Independent fisherman. The Bureau of Indian Affairs financed the purchase of many of these boats for Native residents of Bristol Bay. Statistics taken from Parker, John B. and the Dillingham High School History Class, *The History of Dillingham and Nushagak Bay*, 1973.

Page 80. Discarded sailboats of the Diamond J cannery in 1980. Photo courtesy Karl Ohls.

Pages 81. © Clark James Mishler, 2007

Pages 82 and 83. Wells, circa 1946 B83.91.S156, R17A

Pages 84 and 85. Photo © Bob Waldrop, Red Point Images
Page 86. Quote by John W. Nicholson from his book *No Half Truths: Reminiscences of a Life in Bristol Bay, Alaska, 1906-1995*, Anchorage, Publication Consultants, 1995. Photo courtesy Bob King.

Page 93. Restored PAF sailboat on dock of Peter Pan cannery in Dillingham, AK 2001 looking down Nushagak Bay. Photo courtesy Allen Marquette.

Back Cover. Illustration © Ray Troll

FURTHER READING

In addition to the publications cited in the page notes, the following publications are recommended to the reader who wishes to explore more of the history of commercial fishing in Bristol Bay:

Branson, John, *The Canneries, Cabins and Caches of Bristol Bay*, United States Department of the Interior, Nation Park Service, Lake Clark National Park and Preserve, November 2007.

Ketchum, Robert Glenn and Hampton, Bruce, *Rivers of Life: Southwest Alaska, the Last Great Salmon Fishery*, Aperture 2001.

Van Stone, James, *Eskimos of the Nushagak: An Ethnographic History*, University of Washington Press 1967.

Freeburn, Laurence, *The Silver Years of the Alaska Canned Salmon Industry*, Alaska Geographic, Vol.3, No. 4, 1976.

Andrews, Ralph W. and Larssen, A.K., *Fish and Ships*, Superior Publishing Co., Seattle, 1959.

Lesh, Terry, *Bristol Bay Boats Then and Now*, National Fisherman, May 1982.

You haven't lived until you've pulled a loaded gill net over the stern of a rolling and pitching double-ender in a strong wind. The wind pushes the boat away from the net, and you have to pull the boat upwind and drag the net aboard all at once. Often we had to brace one foot against the splash rail and pull with all our strength. Bristol Bay fishermen had a lot of hernias in those days.

AL ANDREE

Tim Troll came to Alaska in 1978 as a VISTA volunteer lawyer in Bethel. He is currently the Executive Director of the Bristol Bay Heritage Land Trust, a non-profit conservation organization in Bristol Bay with a mission to protect salmon habitat. The material for this book originates in research and interviews he conducted for a radio program called "Our Story" that he produced for KDLG Public Radio in Dillingham.

Every summer I think of Bristol Bay, I remember the past, my friends, my fishing partners, the people from different places in the world I met and worked with, the close calls we had, and the bad and good times. I miss the years I spent there as a young Dena'ina man. It remains an important part of my life.

PETE KOKTELASH

Pacific Alaska Fisheries sailboat restored by Harold Andrew in 2001 for the Samuel K. Fox Museum to celebrate the 100th anniversary of the Peter Pan Cannery in Dillingham.

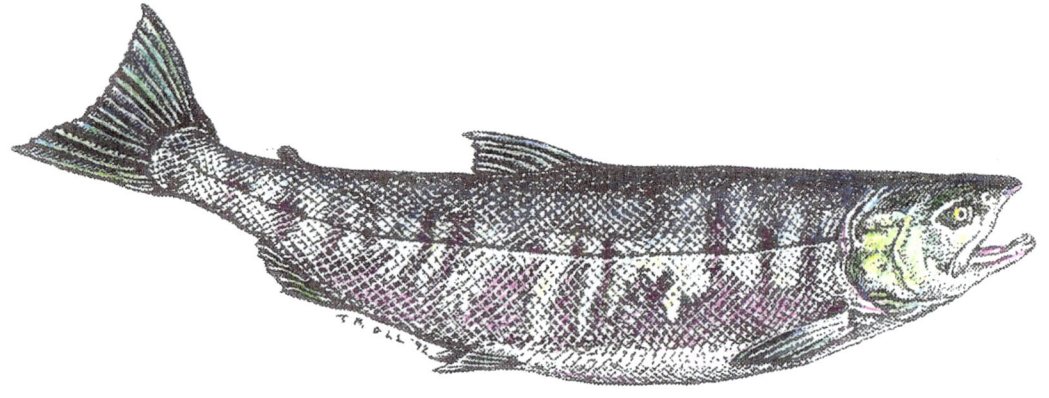

When the dogs show up the season is over.

RAY PADDOCK

www.ingramcontent.com/pod-product-compliance
Lightning Source LLC
Chambersburg PA
CBHW041322290426

44108CB00004B/101